In The

Kingdom

of

The Dalai Lama

In The
Kingdom
of
The Dalai Lama

IN PRINT PUBLISHING
Sedona, Arizona

IN PRINT
PUBLISHING

Published by IN PRINT PUBLISHING
65 Verde Valley School Road # F2
Sedona, Arizona 86336

Editor: Beatrice V. Baker
Cover and Book Design: Fit To Print – Brenda Cossé
Cover Photo: A view of Potala approaching Lhasa from south.

Publisher's Cataloging in Publication

Steele, A.T. (Archibald Trajan), 1903-1992
    In the Kingdom of the Dalai Lama / Archibald T. Steele
    p. cm.
    Preassigned LCCN: 93-09471.
    ISBN 0-9630485-4-6

    1. Tibet (China)--Description and travel. 2. Tibet (China)--
History--1944. I. Title.

DS786.S74 1993   915.5'045
                                             QB193-651

Manufactured in the United States of America
by Griffin Printing

Acknowledgements

I am deeply indebted to His Holiness The Dalai Lama for his personal endorsement; by writing the foreword for this book.

Archibald T. Steele's sister, Isabel Steele and nephew James Steele, were very supportive of my efforts to complete Arch's final project. They both approved and encouraged my endeavors to publish this book, thank you both.

Philip Rulon, Director of History Department at N.A.U., has always taken time from his busy life to encourage and direct me in my projects, thank you dear friend.

I was fortunate to work with Brenda Cossé, Fit To Print, she is an accomplished professional with talent and imagination. She took a personal interest in designing the cover and arranging the contents. Her dedication to the project made it an enjoyable experience.

Tomi Keitlen, In Print Publishing, also took a personal interest in this book. She felt it would have a broader audience than I had envisioned, and has implemented her own valuable experience to the effort. Tomi is well known as a author and in demand as a lecturer.

The Killing of Tibet, by Alex Shoumatoff, was what I needed to dramatize the conditions in Tibet since the Dalai Lama was forced into exile. Thank you Wylie, Aitken & Stone, Inc. for making it possible to include the article.

There are many others that gave encouragement and advice. I am grateful for their help.

THE DALAI LAMA

December 3, 1992

I am happy that Archabald T. Steele's travel writings on Tibet which appeared in 1944 in the Chicago Daily News is now being published in a book form.

It covers the once peaceful country of Tibet as seen through the eyes of the author, who was then a young journalist. In this material, Mr Steele also expresses his concerns about what has happened to Tibet since his trip there.

I regret to note that Mr Steele is no longer with us to share the joy of the completion of his project. However, as desired by the author himself, I am confident that his book will bring to a wider audience the peace and harmony that once prevailed in Tibet prior to the Chinese invasion.

I am also confident that this book will add to the outside world's knowledge and understanding of the unique and rich Tibetan tradition which is under threat.

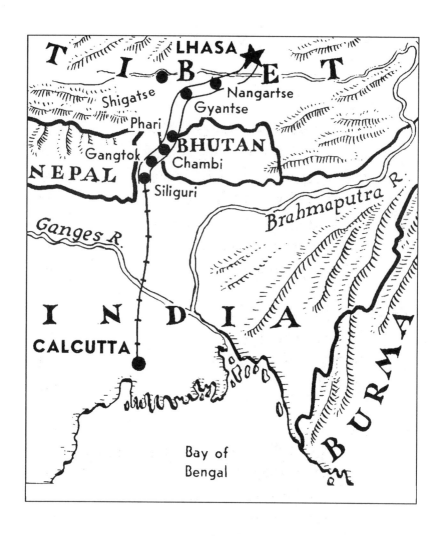

Contents

Prologue

Arch T. Steele

I guess the question most often asked of a foreign correspondent after he retires — at least as far as I was concerned — is, "What was the most exciting experience of your career?" It's been a tough question to answer.

So many of my productive years were spent in hot spot areas covering wars, disasters and world-altering events that now, looking back over that long period of my life, it was a melange of exciting happenings, and I feel fortunate to have participated in those history making events.

I first arrived in Shanghai, always one of the world's most exciting cities, in the midst of a bloody upheaval between the Chinese and Japanese. The untrained Chinese defenders suffered horrendous casualties before being forced to abandon the city. This cruel, uneven contest was my introduction to the senseless devastation of war.

I was to become increasingly familiar in the months and

years ahead with the pain and destruction brought about by greed and passion for power.

I pursued the Chinese war lord Ma Chan-shan through Manchuria, hoping to reach him for a first person interview before the League of Nations closed in. This grueling journey was accomplished by horseback, horse and cart, and on foot across rough and muddy terrain.

I found Mao Tse Tung, the leader of the Communist Revolution in China, in a cave being used as the headquarters, at Yenan deep in North West China. We engaged in a lengthy and intriguing interview. The general was a complicated, dedicated communist.

As time passed, unfortunately, he became increasingly unreasonable and ruthless. He was responsible for the deaths of thousands of young students and intellectuals of all ages during the cultural revolution.

I spent almost a year slowly losing my mind in Stalin's Moscow, following the outbreak of hostilities with Germany. I fought daily battles with the Soviet censors attempting to get my dispatches out of Russia. I do not have fond memories of that period.

I interviewed Mahatma Gandhi, a very wise, intelligent man — truly a holy person — in Bombay. Gandhi was a great influence on the Dalai Lama of Tibet, who refers to him as his mentor.

I watched the signing of the Japanese surrender on the Battleship Missouri at the end of World War II. The total humiliation reflected in the demeanor of the conquered Japanese officers and dignitaries empowered to sign the treaty of surrender intensified the importance of this somber occasion.

In Cairo, with my wife, Esther, we watched the hotel where we were staying burn to the ground, torched by Arab mobs demonstrating against British policies in the Suez Canal Zone. We escaped with our lives; others were not so fortunate.

Surely any of the above adventures would qualify as an exciting experience, however, the experience that made the deepest and most lasting impression was my journey across the Himalayas into forbidden Tibet.

What I saw in Tibet on my visit there in 1944 was an under-developed Shangra La waiting only for the world recognition of its independent status. The little country was at peace with the world.

Sadly, all that has changed. Gone is the talk of Shangri-la. All but forgotten is the dream of an independent Tibet. The fate of Tibet as a self-governing entity is now in dire peril.

My account of this journey, understandably the high point of my career, was serialized in the Chicago Daily News in 1944. My journey was a time of peaceful reflection and acceptance of the differences in religious beliefs and ways of worshiping. All countries and races are attempting to achieve a more perfect life and after-life. This is the underlying quest of all of the people of the world.

My purpose in re-publishing and distributing this story is to renew interest in solving the continuing problem of this beautiful, gentle country.

May it give pleasure and enlightenment.

Arch Steele

On The Way
To The Forbidden City

A passport for Lhasa is hard to obtain. But once it
has been granted, even the savage heights of the
Himalayas seem a minor obstacle.

I had wanted for 12 years to visit the hermit capital of this
land of medieval charm and peerless alpine beauty. Not until
this year did the time seem propitious to make application to
the Tibetan government. The reply came more promptly than I
had expected and was favorable.

The passport was an impressive document two feet square
and of a tough native-made paper. Dated in the Fifth Month of
the Wood-Monkey year, the dozen lines of neat Tibetan calligraphy fixed the route I was to follow and ordered headmen
along the way to accord every reasonable facility to the
American visitor. I was to receive meat, milk, kitchen facilities
and living accommodations when required. The seal of the
Tibetan cabinet — the Kashag — gave authority to the document.

I quickly discovered that going to Lhasa was a vastly more
complicated procedure than any journey I had ever made. I had

A Caravan crossing the Hyapso-la Pass enroute to central Tibet.

to take with me equipment and supplies for a two-month trip. There were gifts to be purchased for the Dalai Lama, the regent and a score of other Tibetan dignitaries.

The things I carried as presents, besides a few pieces of silverware, were simple and inexpensive articles common to us, but hard to get in the remote Tibetan capital — pocketknives, soap, towels, canned fruit, and so forth. Everything was to be transported on the backs of horses and mules, and this required special equipment, numerous adjustments and many eliminations.

Between the headaches of departure, I did a little hasty reading on the nature of the strange land I was getting into. Tibet, I read, is a country 15 times the size of England, with an average elevation of 14,000 feet. It is a land of plateaus and mountains, mostly treeless, and inhabited by something over 6,000,000 people of Mongoloid stock.

Its Buddhist inhabitants, said the almanacs, are ruled by a priest-king — the Dalai Lama — and are intensely devoted to their religion; one out of every three male Tibetans is a monk. They are a race of herdsmen and small farmers controlled, on completely feudal lines, by a few score families of wealth, title and culture.

Tibet, I learned, is the land of the horse, the yak and the donkey. Nobody rides trains, automobiles or airplanes, because there aren't any. Another point no writer overlooked was that Tibetans probably drank more tea per capita than any people in the world — 30 to 80 cups a day. I later confirmed this. I don't care if I ever see another cup of tea.

Equipped with these homely facts and masses of useful

and useless paraphernalia, tourist Steele entrained from Calcutta. It was an overnight journey to the junction of Siliguri, at the base of the Himalayan foothills.

An automobile carried me 70 miles further, through the jungled precipitous Tista valley to the hilltop village of Gangtok, capital of the border state of Sikkim. Landslides had wiped out the road at two points, but it was a simple matter to walk the five miles between them. For a few silver rupees and a package of cigarettes, Nepalese road workers willingly left their job and lugged my baggage.

At the Sikkimese capital, 5,500 feet up, friends advised me to acclimate myself for a few days before starting over the Himalayan passes. I laughed off advice, but regretted it later.

I called on the Maharaja of Sikkim. Like all Sikkimese, Tibetan, British and Chinese officials I met along the way, he was friendly and hospitable. Of Tibetan stock, he is the ruler of 125,000 rice-growing hill people in a tiny state where elevations run from almost sea level to the dazzling pinnacle of Kanchenjunga (28,000 feet), the world's third highest mountain.

Through the years an influx of Nepalese immigrants has greatly diluted Sikkim's racial affinity to Tibet. But the ruling house has retained its racial purity. It is an inflexible custom for members of the maharaja's family to marry only members of the Tibetan nobility. The maharaja's two daughters, known everywhere by their nicknames. "Coo-Coo" and "Kula," are famed in this border region for their charm and beauty. One is the wife of a Lhasa official, the other is unmarried.

The British raj exercises a gentle but firm supervision over the affairs of Sikkim through an able political officer, Sir Basil

Heavily loaded pilgrims on trail to Lhasa.

Gould. For the British, this frontier state with its numerous family connections in Lhasa is a useful bridge to Tibet proper.

On the morning of the third day in Gangtok, I unsteadily mounted a horse and started the long trans-Himalayan journey which was to land me in Lhasa three weeks later.

It is a 314-mile horseback journey from Gangtok, in the Himalayan foothills, to Lhasa, in the heart of Tibet. You cross four skyscraping passes, ranging from 14,300 to 16,400 feet. For all but a few days of the trip you are traveling at elevations higher than 12,000 feet.

It sounds pretty formidable, but it really isn't. Anybody with an abnormally rugged heart and a durable seat can do it. It is true that for a city feller like myself, who had never ridden anything harder than the rear seat of a Jeep, two months of daily contact with the backs of Tibetan ponies was a little wearing.

But the strange, beautiful, sometimes incredible sights of Tibet and its sacred capital more than compensated for the physical discomforts.

Nor was it necessary, as I had half expected, to sleep in the open, shiver in my sleeping bag or roast mutton over an open camp fire. For slightly more than half the distance to Lhasa along this much-traveled caravan route between India and Tibet the British have built comfortable rest-houses at the end of each march.

Your servant arrives about an hour ahead of you, spreads the alarm that a sahib is coming, and by the time you get there a cozy fire is burning in the fireplace and a pot of tea is waiting to warm your innards.

These bungalows are well-stocked with ancient maga-

Tibetan pilgrims on trail to Lhasa.

zines. You can put yourself to sleep with the dull humor of a 1926 copy of Punch. The mantelpiece is adorned with pictures calculated to remind wandering Britons that home is heaven after all — peaceful British scenes entitled "St. George's Day at East Burdleigh, Devon," "Field Marguerites near Barcombe, Sussex," and the like.

Nevertheless, the weary traveler thanks Providence and the British for these little cottages appearing suddenly at the end of the day, in the most out-of-the-way places.

At Gyantse, Tibet's third largest town, nine stages (133 miles) from Lhasa, the zone of British influence abruptly ends.

From there on, you either camp out or stay in Tibetan houses. I preferred the houses. The kindly villagers invariably installed me in the room of worship — the best in the house — where fierce and benign images of the Buddhist gods stared down on me from their cubicles along the wall.

Horses were changed at almost every halt. They were recruited by the headmen from peasants of their villages. At the beginning there were seven horses in my caravan — a rather small show, by Tibetan standards. Three were saddle horses for my two servants and myself. The others were loaded down with bedrolls, kitchen utensils, foodstuffs, presents and even 40 pounds of silver coins, with which to pay off those Tibetans (and there are plenty of them) who don't trust paper money.

My right-hand man, like many Tibetans, was named after the day of the week on which he was born. That happened to be "Pa-sang"—Friday. His brother-in-law, the cook, was "Norbhu" (Jewel).

Pa-sang was one of the most widely-traveled Tibetans I have met. As personal servant to a British officer, he had toured England, Scotland and France.

Yet his faith in the gods of his ancestors was unshaken. He never passed a prayer-wheel without turning it. The trip to Lhasa was for him a pilgrimage. His obeisances to the gilded deities were as deep and respectful as those of any other good Buddhist.

For the first four stages, I had an amiable traveling companion in Rai Sahib Sonam, a Sikkimese serving as British trade agent in Yatung. He unlocked many Tibetan mysteries for me.

From Gangtok, in India, we plodded upward for two and

A Tibetan pilgrim along the trail. He holds in his hand a prayer wheel which he turns constantly. The wheel is full of printed Tibetan prayers. You gain merit by spinning the wheel.

a half days over a good trail, toward the first of the high passes—Natu-la—at the frontier of Tibet. Past 10,000 feet we emerged from the jungle with its orchids and leeches into a zone of cedars and firs.

At 13,000, near the sterile alpine lake of Changu, we entered the bleak, final climb to the summit, through a stony

skyland where only rhododendrons, wild rhubarb and a variety of hardy plants, including the beautiful Himalayan poppy, made a stand.

Tibetan inscriptions on the rocks and prayer flags over the waterfalls and bridges reminded us that we were nearing Lamaland. At the pass itself, a saddle-like depression between splintered crags, the Tibetans with me tossed stones onto a flag-covered pile made by generations of Tibetans before them and invoked the blessings of the gods.

"God should always win; the devil should always lose!" they shouted.

A thin spiral of sweet-smelling smoke rose from an offering of incense ignited by an earlier traveler. Behind us clouds of steamy mist boiled up from the plains of India as from a monstrous cauldron. Ahead of us, the Chumbi valley, studded with stately pines, fell away to dark depths. We crossed the ridge and were in Tibet.

Crossing the bleak Natu Pass in Tibet, we overtook straggling processions of perspiring men, women and children burdened with supplies for blockaded China. They were porters of several races — Nepalese, Sikkimese, Tibetans — slight of build but with leg muscles that bulged out of proportion to their bodies. Most carried the standard load of about 83 pounds. A few staggered under twice that weight.

We asked one little Nepalese coolie with 166 pounds on his back how he did it. Before answering, he took a long draw on the cigarette I had proffered him.

"When the pay is good, the load seems light. Men and horses are scarce, so the Chinese must give a high price for our work. For carrying this load from Gangtok to Yatung I will get 30 rupees ($9). That's a lot of money for four days work, even if it means climbing this big mountain."

Materials for China are today the biggest item in the caravan traffic from India into Tibet. It takes them three to four months to make the arduous crossing of the great Tibetan land barrier. There is a shortage of pack animals on the Indian frontier, so the stuff is transported for the first few stages on the backs of coolies.

Once the Tibetan plateau is reached, yaks, horses and donkeys take over. There are two or three trans-Tibetan caravan routes to China, but this one carries most of the traffic. Yet the total tonnage of all of them barely exceeds 2,000 tons annually, less than 1 percent of the airborne traffic over the famous

"Hump."

These caravan trails to China carry commercial goods only and are utilized by merchants unable to get their merchandise into China by air. With the air traffic confined almost exclusively to high priority war materials, private traders have no choice but the difficult Tibetan back door. The transport cost is appalling — averaging about one dollar a pound for the haul across Tibet. But that does not prevent the Chinese importers from making fantastic profits.

All the way along the up-and-down trail to Lhasa and back I passed great China-bound caravans, usually escorted by picturesque riflemen. If they were not on the move, they were encamped — the cargo piled high, as a wind-break around the black yak-hair tents of the Tibetan drivers. The animal-borne freight consisted largely of cloth from the mills of India, packed in dark jute-bound bales.

Textiles of any kind are in great demand in China, where they command enormous prices. I noticed that the returning caravans were loaded with wool, Tibet's major export. Virtually all of it is destined, if shipping can be obtained, for the United States. Tibetan wool is used in America for making carpets and upholstering automobile seats.

But I am getting ahead of my story. Mountain sickness hit me a few hours after we had crossed Natu Pass. It is an unpleasant combination of nausea, headache and high fever. We spent the night at the alpine bungalow of Chumbithang, but when servants told me weird stories of an English lady who had died there several years before and of servants' quarters that were haunted, I decided that neither they nor I were going to be

A monk prostrating himself from Punaka, in Bhutan,
to Shigatse, in Tibet.

happy there. So I moved on next morning, fever and all, toward Yatung, first important village in Tibet, and at a healthfully lower elevation than Chumbithang.

We came upon the one figure of a man moving across country by the slow and tedious process of prostration. He would fall to his knees, sprawl to his full length, then rise to his feet in the place where his hands had reached. He repeated the routine, each time progressing the length of his body.

He proved to be a monk who was prostrating himself from Punaka, in Bhutan, to Shigatse, in Tibet — about 300 miles — obliging him to crawl over the Himalayas. He expected that the whole pilgrimage would take him three or four months. (This illustrates the photograph published on the cover of NEWS VIEWS today.)

To protect his hands from wear and tear he wore wooden clappers. A leather apron shielded his body and knees. Like most monks he had no money but depended for food and shelter on offerings from Buddhists along the way.

Halfway down the steep slope of the Chumbi valley, a Tibetan monastery showed up through the pines. Two red-robed monks, who had heard the jingling bells of our caravan afar off, stood on a balcony blowing fog-horn notes of welcome from 10-foot trumpets. To me, they sounded like the trumpets of Gabriel. The abbot and several of his staff waited at the ornate gate to invite us in for a cup of tea. But I was in no condition even for tea.

At Yatung, a village of square, solid houses, I accepted the warm hospitality of Rai Sahib Sonam and went to bed for four days. I had callers. One of them was the Tibetan trade agent, magnificently gowned in yellow Chinese silk and wearing a conical, gold-tipped hat, set with a turquoise of striking size and color.

He was much concerned, he said, over the problem of marketing Tibetan wool in the United States. He wondered if it wouldn't be possible for Tibetans to do business directly with American manufacturers and so deprive the middleman in India of their pound of flesh. I was unable to enlighten him.

The High Road
To Fabulous Shangri-la

My caravan was joined at Yatung by two Tibetan soldiers assigned by the government of Lhasa. Their orders were to escort me to the holy capital and return. Like all Tibetans, they were devoutly religious. On the trail the chanting of their prayers often mingled with the clump of hooves and the jingle of bells. Their burden of rifles, knives and umbrellas was made more cumbersome by the Buddhist images and charms they carried in ornate metal cases hung from their shoulders.

The military escorts served a useful purpose. One went ahead with my passport in hand to cajole headmen into providing horses promptly. This sometimes took more than simple cajolery, however. At least once, as I learned later, a horsewhip was used. The second soldier stayed with the pack train to guard it against thievery.

I carried no weapons, but I soon began to wonder if I was the only traveler in Tibet who did not have either a rifle or a sword. Even wandering monks, of whom there were many on the trail, frequently bore rude spears for their self-protection.

Pair of Nepalese porters on Natu-la.
Observe extreme youth of boy in foreground.

Along the road we saw interesting examples of antique firearms tipped at the muzzle with antelope horns, the better to steady them when a bead is being taken.

Despite this display of armament, nobody gave us trouble on the trail. Caravans are seldom molested.

At Yatung, a procession of porters came one day to my house with presents from the Tibetan trade agent. They brought on trays, a whole dried sheep, several dozen eggs and a quantity of yak butter. This was repeated at most of the big towns through which I passed.

The presentation was usually made by the headman and was always accompanied by a white scarf, which in Tibet signifies purity of friendship. The meat was often pretty high, the eggs were generally old and the butter was always slightly rancid. But the Tibetans like it that way.

While traveling with Rai Sahib Sonam — my host in Yatung — I observed that people of humble status usually greeted him by taking off their hats, bowing their heads and protruding their tongues. If they were on horseback they dismounted. In speaking they would often suck in their words as though it were a sin to pollute the surrounding air. These are the traditional signs of respect shown by ordinary Tibetans for officers and priests of rank.

From Yatung, deep in the Chumbi valley, we urged our horses steadily upward for two days toward the crest of the Himalayas, over a trail thickly studded with rocks of cobblestone size. In the lower valleys we passed irrigated fields of barley, tiny villages and the inevitable monasteries.

High above them, clinging precariously to the steep

slope, were hermitages where merit-seeking monks lived in voluntary solitary confinement for weeks, for years, even for lifetimes.

At one such retreat, which I visited later, a monk had just emerged after 20 years of meditation, isolation and semidarkness. He had seen no human being and talked to no one in that time. Food was passed to him through a hole in the wall by devout villagers, who gained merit themselves by contributing food to the holy man. The hermit reciprocated by giving a little ball of barley flour, blessed by him, to each donor. He did not show his face. Only his arm appeared through the aperture.

The canyon narrowed and the little fields gave way to dense forest and stark cliffs. And finally the woods were behind us and we were entering the grasslands of the Tibetan plateau. The gigantic, snow-capped mass of Chomolhari (Queen of the Divine Hills) towered above us on the right.

Sacred to every Tibetan, this 24,000-foot monument of nature guards the gateway to Tibet like Gibraltar magnified a thousand times. At its base lies Tang-la, second of the high passes on the road to Lhasa.

The final ascent is over an easy, gentle slope of treeless grassland swept almost continuously by a strong south wind. It is a hard wind but a dry one. The heavy cargo of moisture with which it started from India has been pretty well wrung out by the lower peaks en route. Once you have crossed the Tang-la you are over the Himalayan rampart, but still higher passes lie ahead.

A few miles short of the crest we came upon the town of Phari, a collection of stone and sod houses called by some travelers "the highest, windiest, dirtiest town in the world."

But the squalor of the place is overshadowed by the feudal splendor of the ancient fort that stands over it.

People in Phari live in houses built below the level of the streets and surround themselves with walls of sod as protection against the biting winds of winter. I spent the night there and the next morning went over to the Tang-la.

The highlands of Tibet are the biggest fish and game preserve in the world. It is an offense against Tibetan Buddhism to take life, so wild animals are permitted to roam and multiply almost unmolested over the greater part of this upland kingdom.

Tibetans believe that every living creature is a reincarnation of some previous existence and will be reincarnated in a new form after death. The form that you will take depends on the kind of life you lead. The more merit you build up in this life the better your chances of being reborn on a higher plane.

This is one of many reasons why Tibetans are so disinterested in the material outer world with its wars and its machines. Nirvana, they say, does not lie in that direction.

Traveling across the windy uplands beyond Phari, we observed gazelles in large numbers, feeding and disporting themselves near the trail. Wild donkeys and mountain sheep are commonly seen. On the Rham Tso, an alpine lake, wild ducks and geese are to be counted not by the hundreds but by the tens of thousands. Hawks, fish eagles and lone specimens of that majestic giant of the skies, the lammergeier (a huge vulture), refused to budge from their rocky perches, though we passed within a few yards.

Boldest and sauciest of all were the Tibetan ravens, the

Himalayan Mountain chain from Phari Plain. Central peak is Chomolhari, sacred to Tibetans. Although photograph gives the impression of nearness, the peaks are actually many miles distant across the other side of a wide valley.

ubiquitous scavengers of the Tibetan plateau. At every camp they greeted us with their raucous cries, and often along the road. They would dart daringly to within a few feet to snatch morsels of food. Their chief competitors were the dogs. Tibet is full of dogs. Every household, every caravan has one or more — often so fierce that they have to be kept on a rope. The prevailing breed is a huge, shaggy, bearlike beast not unlike a St. Bernard but with a black coat and a foul temper. A doctor in Gyantse told me that one of the most common complaints was dog bite.

As you pass through Tibetan villages dogs bark at you from all sides, not only at your feet but from rooftops and walls. The wise traveler stays on his horse until he has reconnoitered the canine situation.

The ban on hunting is by no means complete, except near

the holy places. In remote regions shepherds pick off an occasional deer or gazelle for food. Hunting by Europeans is tolerated in some areas along the trade route, although most trekkers entering Tibet are obliged to sign a pledge to do no hunting or fishing.

There is a British official up here who hunts geese with a slingshot. It's not as difficult as it sounds. Wild pigeons are numerous and make good eating if your meat supply is running low. At one bungalow where I stayed a traveler arrived carrying three pigeons that he had killed along the trail. Another bird was needed to round out a good meal for all of us. Just before supper a servant stopped in to announce there was a pigeon outside the door. The traveler stepped to the door, fired and was back in his chair in three minutes. Not very sporting, perhaps, but our meal was complete.

Later in our journey we encountered a flock of gray geese and Brahmani ducks feeding beside the trail. My cook, though a good Buddhist, could not resist the temptation to toss a stone at a potential goose dinner. His aim was good and the feathers flew, but the geese took to flight. They settled down again a few yards away and nonchalantly resumed their feeding.

Despite their antipathy to killing, the Tibetans are great meat eaters. The climate necessitates it. Mutton shares place with parched barley flour and Tibetan tea as one of the three mainstays of the Tibetan diet. They kill sheep in the fall, dry the meat and make it last a year.

In Lhasa the slaughtering and butchering is done by people of low caste. Sheep killed for the Dalai Lama's table are always blessed beforehand so that the animals will be assured of a decent break in the next incarnation. Passing through Tibet I saw hundreds of yaks and sheep with woolly tassels hanging from perforations in their ears. These are animals dedicated to Buddha, which means they will never be killed.

The shaggy yak — remotely similar in appearance to the American bison — is the beast of all purposes in Tibet. It pulls the plough and carries the loads. It provides meat, milk and cheese. Its hair makes tough rope and waterproof tenting. And yak dung is the standard fuel of Tibet, serving the same purposes as did buffalo chips for our ancestors on America's Western plains.

Many Tibetan lakes and rivers are teeming with fish, but nobody bothers them. Insects too, enjoy a charmed life. There are fundamentalist priests who will not venture from their

Herd of yaks carrying freight from India to Lhasa.

Tang Pass in the Himalayas.

monasteries at certain times of the year for fear of inadvertently stepping on insects.

At the Tang pass the Himalayas take a turn to the north. For three days, as we jogged across the high grass country, the great peaks passed us on the right like a stately procession of white-gowned nuns behind the protecting bulk of their majestic leader, Chomolhari. The latter, though a mountain of many moods, was at her best when she wore the misty halo of some stratospheric tempest.

Nature has been prodigal with the spectacular in these Asiatic highlands. Here are so many mountains of 20,000 feet or over that many are unnamed and most are unclimbed. Here are huge expanses of virgin grazing ground never scratched by a plow but marked occasionally by little oasis of darker green where man has found water enough to plant struggling stands of barley, peas and mustard. Little else will thrive at these lofty altitudes, although I found solitary willows almost up to 15,000 feet.

The high road to Lhasa skirts several alpine lakes of impressive size, fed by the numerous Himalayan glaciers. One of them, Yamdrok Tso (Lake of the Upper Pastures), has the brilliant blue-green coloration of liquid turquoise.

Villages were five to 20 miles apart, often with nothing between. Their thick-walled turreted buildings, with prayer flags fluttering in the eternal breeze, loomed up with deceptive clarity long before we reached them. They are of squarish, fortress-like construction — stone, adobe brick or even sod — with high outer walls and narrow windows. These rugged features are more for defense against wind and cold than against possible intruders.

For 50 miles my little caravan skirted the northern shadow of the Himalayas through trails worn deep in the close-cropped grassland. Then we veered off into a series of small cultivated valleys leading down to the plain and citadel of Gyantse. At Gyantse I was slightly more than halfway to Lhasa.

Built like most Tibetan towns, around a rocky prominence surmounted by a massive fort, Gyantse looked like something out of a medieval landscape. In the shadow of the castle lay a monastery. Its golden-roofed chorten and its high outer walls, snaking along the rocky ridges, added to the effect.

Inside the town and its busy bazaar I found the customary squalor of almost any Oriental marketplace. Gyantse is the third-largest city of Tibet, but I doubt if its population exceeds 10,000. Here the trade route from India branches. The main road goes on to Lhasa. Another trail veers westward toward Shigatse, Tibet's second largest town and seat of the Panchen Lama (when there is one.)

By treaty with the Tibetans the British trade agents have escorts of Indian troops at Gyantse and Yatung. But this is the limit of British military representation. Gyantse is the end, too, of the British post and telegraph system from India. The postal system consists of a remarkably efficient pony — or, rather, mule — express, operating in relays from India. Even the British cannot go beyond Gyantse without permission from Lhasa, and this is very hard to get. Most British commandants in Gyantse complete their tour of duty without ever seeing Lhasa, though it is only 133 miles away.

Here I met Sir Basil Gould, who was en route to Lhasa on a special mission. Here also were Cyril Finch, the British trade agent, and Dr. M.V. Kurian, the garrison physician. Gould was leaving in the morning for Lhasa. He invited me to accompany him for a few days.

Somehow the beggars of the town got wind of the impending departure of the big British sahib. When we mounted our horses in the morning there they were, lining the road with hands outstretched. Custom dictates that a departing guest must remember the poor. Sir Basil and his staff were not neglectful of the ways of the country. Coins rained on the pleading mendicants as we rode past.

The First Glimpse
of Golden Roofs

The Chicago Daily News expedition to Lhasa, with its seven spavined nags, was all but lost in the vastly bigger one of Sir Basil Gould. The British political officer was proceeding to the Tibetan capital with 200 pony-loads of equipment, supplies and presents. The animals were strung out along many miles of trail.

Sir Basil is an institution on the Tibetan frontier. As political agent for Sikkim and Bhutan he is also a sort of steward for British political and commercial interests in Tibet. It is a job which requires consummate tact and delicate handling and is complicated by Anglo-Chinese rivalry for Tibet's favor.

Gould was a generous host. He provided me with a tent and loaned me a horse in place of the decrepit creature I had been riding. He himself rode a mule, an animal favored also by Tibetans because of its sure-footedness and fast, ambling gait.

The Gould party consisted of an Indian doctor, Sikkimese clerks, Bhutanese grooms, Mohammedan servants, Tibetan translators, an official Tibetan guide, Tibetan soldiers, and a small army of drivers and coolies, some accompanied by their womenfolk and children. It was a polyglot but impressive procession. Tents and equipment went ahead, so that when we came to a halting place, our little tent city was up and ready for us.

The Indian garrison at Gyantse gave Gould a mounted guard of honor as far as the mansion of Raja Tering, seven miles out. The silk-gowned raja, who is a brother of the Maharaja of Sikkim and might have had the Sikkimese throne himself had he not preferred the life of a Tibetan squire, regaled us with a Tibetan meal served in the Chinese manner. The raja is one of Britain's good friends in Tibet.

We dropped our Indian escort and moved on through irrigated valleys, over quaint bridges, across open grassland and

Tibetan soldiers (color-bearers).

finally to the third and highest pass on the road to Lhasa — the 16,400-foot Kharo-la.

The Tibetans of the caravan shouted their praise to Buddha as we passed through the rude archway of sticks and prayer flags at the barren summit. It was an easy crossing through a depression between peaks 24,000 feet high.

Archway of stones and prayer flags over the 16,400 foot pass of Kharo-la, on the road to Lhasa.

From the mighty mass of the sacred mountain No-jin Kang-sang, on our left, a hanging glacier sprawled downward to within 1,000 feet of the trail. Blocks of ice as big as houses, forced up by gigantic pressures, were silhouetted on its upper surface like monstrous battlements. Icicles 50 feet long hung from snowy cliffs.

A day later we came to the castled town of Nangartse, on the shore of Yamdrok Lake. Tibetan dignitaries, doing honor to their official British guest, met us three miles out in the traditional manner and exchanged scarves.

Five miles away, atop a lonely hill overlooking the lake, sits the ancient monastery of Sam Ding, ruled by a 7-year-old girl. This child is believed by Tibetans to be the incarnation on earth of the goddess Dorji Phamu ("Thunderbolt Sow") and is thought to have the power of converting herself into a pig. One of her predecessors is claimed to have done so. There are several hundred incarnation lamas in Tibet, but the girl at Sam Ding is the only female incarnation. She is the holiest person of her sex in the country.

Dr. Kurian and I, with a Sikkimese official, took to our saddles and rode across the marshy plain to Sam Ding to meet this remarkable child. We carried as gifts an umbrella, a towel and a few bars of perfumed soap. At the hilltop we passed under a stuffed yak overhanging the monastery entrance and climbed a precipitous flight of steps to the cavernous room, hung with Buddhist paintings, in which the female deity presided over the affairs of some 65 monks.

The girl sat on a throne, wrapped in maroon robes and white silk, and attended by the only woman in the monastery — a middle-aged, shorn-headed nun.

The child seemed frail but pretty, with high cheekbones and bright little eyes that gazed at us solemnly. The Tibetans and Sikkimese prostrated themselves at the girl's feet. After the usual blessing, we were presented with packages of pills and incense blessed by the goddess and believed to be especially efficacious in driving out devils.

On our return to Nangartse, we brought ourselves back to reality by listening to the news of the world broadcast from London, through Gould's radio. You need something like this occasionally in Tibet to remind you that you are still an inhabitant of that planet called Earth.

The world you had known seems a million miles away. Gould's radio always drew a fascinated Tibetan audience. The look on their faces when the noise box produced an American crooner's rendition of "He Says 'Murder', He Says," is something I will never forget. They thought it was crazy — and who is to say they were wrong!

When the Tibetan interpreter saw the itinerary I had mapped out for the remainder of my trip to Lhasa, he consulted his Tibetan calendar and frowned. It seemed that I had picked an unlucky day for my arrival in the Holy City, and that would never do. It would give offense to my Tibetan hosts, I must choose a more auspicious day.

I took his advice, postponed my arrival, and had reason, later, to be glad of it. Tibetans are sensitive to breaches of etiquette.

I left the caravan of Sir Basil Gould at Nangartse, with the intention of doing the rest of the trip to Lhasa in four days. For 20 miles the trail clung closely to that bluest of all lakes, the Yamdrok Tso, then turned steeply upward toward the misty, 16,000-foot summit of Nyapso-la, last of the passes. It was hard, rough going, over a very rocky trail, and our tired ponies paused frequently for breath. A down-coming herd of yaks, blundering all over the mountainside, did not make it any easier.

At the top of the grassy divide we were rewarded with an unforgettable sight. On the side from which we had come, the azure-hued Yamdrok Lake twisted in and out through the hills to the base of the ghostly Himalayas, barely visible on the southern horizon. Before us, on the north side of the divide, lay the deep valley of the upper Brahmaputra River, known to Tibetans as the Tsang-po. This brown torrent, impressively big even here, courses for hundreds of miles along the north side of the Himalayan rampart, seeking a way out, until at last, at the northeastern tip of India, it finds a breach and plunges through it into Assam, Bengal, the Ganges and the sea.

We dismounted and led our weary animals down the steep slope of the dividing ridge. I was reminded of a Tibetan saying which I had read, I think, in a book by Sir Charles Bell:

"If he cannot carry you up the hill, he is no horse; if you cannot walk down the hill, you are no man."

I spent the night in the house of a Tibetan farmer, close to the Brahmaputra's banks. He came with a gift of milk and peaches, the latter no bigger than walnuts. But these peaches were evidence that we had descended into a region of greater fertility and milder climate. The Brahmaputra, here, has cut its way down to the 12,000-foot level, a low elevation in Tibet.

The farmhouse where I stayed was of a pattern that became very familiar to me before my journey was over. The ground floor, as usual, was reserved for animals. The household occupied the second story, reached by a steep, ladderlike stair-way. They busied themselves about the dark, mud-floored rooms, spinning and weaving wool, churning butter, preparing tea, and just gossiping. The guest room, where I stayed, was

Tibetan peasant woman.

also the room of the family shrine. Walls and ceilings were lined with faded patterned cloth. On one side was a row of gilded cabinets, embossed with dragons and phoenixes in the Chinese manner, and containing the family valuables. Along the top of the cabinet, some 15 Buddhist images peered out from little decorated alcoves. Most were of gilded clay. The many-armed Chenrezi was there, so was the Buddha, so was the fierce household god. Against another wall were more cabinets and boxes of wood and rawhide, fastened with ponderous Tibetan padlocks. Aging photographs of the late Dalai Lama and the defunct Panchen Lama adorned colorfully decorated pillars supporting the rafters.

Glass is expensive in Tibet, because it has to be imported

from India, so the single window was without it. Against the window was a low couch, covered with a decorative rug and overhung by a square canopy of tattered silk. The rugs on the floor were clean but threadbare.

From the window I was able to overlook the walled court-yard, which toward evening was full of the bustle of arriving caravans. Horses and donkeys were driven in for unloading and feeding. Cows and calves came in from the fields. A large dog, looking all the fiercer for the woolly red collar around its neck, was tied near the entrance and greeted every arrival with a burst of deep-throated barking. On the roof of a stable across the yard, a group of Tibetan urchins gazed at my window, straining for a glimpse of the strange foreigner. Peasants from neighboring farms had been called into the compound for a fatherly talk from the headman on the duties expected of them. They nodded acquiescence to all his remarks with the cheerful humility of feudal serfs.

The relation of landlord and peasant is such in Tibet that the former is empowered, if he wishes, to punish recalcitrant tenants by whipping or even confinement.

Lhasa was near, and the journey was easier. For 15 miles I floated down the Brahmaputra in a yak-skin boat. It was a clumsy, box-like coracle, made of four yak hides sewn together and stretched over a frame of willow saplings. It looked awfully frail, at first, but my confidence grew as we bobbed through the rapids without incident.

The boatman, a leathery-faced Tibetan in ragged, home-spun woolens, guided the boat — if you can call it that — from the stern with a couple of crudely-fashioned oars. He said he had been plying this river for 40 years and that made me feel better, too. The coracle is good only for downstream work. At his destination, the boatman takes his craft from the water, balances it on his back and trudges with it back along the river bank to his starting point. One day down, three days back — that's the routine.

We had a bigger passenger list than I expected. Various pilgrims, attracted, no doubt, by the power of our passport, had attached themselves to our caravan en route. Now they converged on my yak-skin liner for a free ride down-river. It gave me a chance to get acquainted. Among them were a Tibetan monk and a Chinese trader, both on a pilgrimage, so they said, to the shrines of Lhasa. They chanted prayers all the way down river. The boatman kept time to the rhythmic intonations. "Om mani padme hum!" ("Hail The Jewel on the Lotus.") "Om mani padme hum!" I was soon chanting it myself.

Drifting along this mountain-flanked waterway, under a blazing sun, we passed much of interest. A great monastery crowded the water's edge. Others hugged the hills. Villages stood in the terraced ravines, where flourishing crops of barley and wheat were watered by melting snows from the higher peaks. There were ruined forts, crumbling watchtowers and Buddhist monuments, some of them relics of Tibet's earliest historical epoch of small warring principalities. At points where the shoreline took some strange configuration or where the river broke into rapids there were the inevitable prayer flags. And ever so often a procession of what appeared to be huge, two-legged beetles would be seen moving along the shore. They were simply boats like ours, being carried up river, but they

*Approaching Lhasa, the magnificent winter palace of the Dalai Lama,
also called the Potala, provides an inspiring view. Below it, on the
plain, sprawls the town of Lhasa, of which only a part is visible here.*

enhanced the out-of-this-world illusion that you often get while
traveling in Tibet.

In early afternoon we reached another of those high-
perched forts, or "dzongs," so characteristic of this country. At
its base was the village of Chu-shui, where we were to put up
for the night. Lhasa was only a day and a half away, up the flat,
gravelly valley of the Kyi Chu, one of the Brahmaputra's tribu-
taries. Our coracle could go no further. Such boats can come
down the Kyi Chu, but they cannot go up. Later, on leaving
Lhasa, I was to make that 30-mile water trip. On that occasion,

we had an extra passenger — a sheep. On the overland uptrip, the boatman carries the coracle, but the sheep, jogging faithfully behind, packs his master's food and bedding.

As we neared Lhasa, on fresh horses, we encountered numerous evidences of our approach to what Tibetans call the "City of the Gods." Cairns of stones and rock inscriptions became more frequent. The words "Om mani padme hum" have been chiseled for eternity into thousands, perhaps tens of thousands of rocks in Tibet by worshipful Buddhists seeking merit. Words of praise to the Dalai Lama have been written in white-washed gravel on more than one mountainside. Conspicuous stone faces near the trail often bear carved likenesses of Tibetan deities.

Eight miles from Lhasa I caught the first glint, across the plain, of the gleaming, golden roofs of the Potala, struck by a shaft of sunlight, at the foot of the distant hills. The spectacle grew as we drew nearer. Three miles away I was met by my good friend of Chungking days, Hugh Richardson, temporarily in charge of the British mission in Lhasa. We rode in together, under the noon sun, with the outer beauties of the hermit capital gradually unveiling themselves before us — the massive pile of the Potala dominating all and fronted by the hill of the Temple of Medicine, its rocky arms thrown out in protective embrace. Between these two heights could be glimpsed the flat roofs and the white-washed houses of the town of Lhasa.

After 21 days on the trail, this seemed to me the most welcome and stirring panorama I had ever seen.

Monk trumpeters calling worshippers to prayer. Potala in distance.

A Pilgrim Meets "The Presence"

Religion is everything in Tibet, I was often reminded of this on the long journey from India. During my two weeks in Lhasa, the hermit capital, I was not able to forget it for a minute.

The Tibetan government provided me with a little house in a park of gnarled willows, down by the river. It was a small square building of thick stone walls, previously used as a retreat by Lhasa picnickers. It had been empty; but for my benefit, partitions and a few pieces of furniture had been installed. Across the entrance hung a black curtain of yak-hair cloth.

I had hardly settled in, when a line of porters arrived bringing gifts of foodstuffs from the government. They included two sheep, two raw-hide bags filled with Bhutanese rice, several dozen eggs of rare vintage, quantities of butter, flour and horse-feed. Similar contributions came from the prime minister. It was evident that the government did not intend to let its guest go hungry.

My first call was on the foreign office. There I met Surkhang Dzaza, the shrewd and personable chief of the department, and Ringang Kusho, one of the very few Tibetans educated in England. Custom dictated that my meeting with the Dalai Lama could not take place in less than three days after my arrival. But as the third day happened to be a Saturday—the Dalai Lama's unlucky day—I would have to wait until the fourth. In the meantime, I was told, it would not be proper to make any other formal calls. I could fill the time seeing the sights of Lhasa.

To assist me as guide and interpreter, the foreign office assigned a young English-speaking member of the aristocracy, George Tsarong. He proved an infallible and indispensable advisor in the complexities of Tibetan etiquette. Good manners mean much in Lhasa, and if you don't observe the prevailing conventions you soon lose more face than you can afford.

Lhasa lies in the neck of a fertile valley, rimmed on three sides by bare mountains running up to 19,000 feet. The town itself sits at an elevation of but 12,000 feet, so that for Tibet its climate is reasonably temperate. There is little rain, less snow, much sunshine, meadows, parks and fields of wheat and barley surround the town. In Lhasa, you are never out of sight of the Potala, one of the architectual wonders of the world. To erect this great pile even with the primitive tools available in Tibet today, would be a gigantic feat. Several centuries ago, it must have seemed a miracle. The Potala is a sprawling fortress-like mass of many hundreds of rooms surmounting the summit of a low hill. Fifteen stories high, in places, it appears to lean against the hill's summit, and some believe that this is the clue to its architectural secret. There is no steel in its construction.

Temples, chortens, monuments, palaces and the mansions

Steele's monk guide in Lhasa.

of wealthy Tibetan officials also stud the Lhasa landscape, but they are all dwarfed by the Potala's vast bulk against the northern sky.

Lhasa town is a collection of close-packed buildings intersected by a maze of narrow, tortuous streets. There is no sewage system, so most refuse goes into the street. Dogs and ravens are the scavengers. Were it not for the altitude, Lhasa might have a serious disease problem. But flies don't thrive at this altitude and epidemics are rare.

In the bazaar district there are many small shops stocked with the simple needs of the Tibetan villager and peasant. Cloth from India and brick tea from China, brought at great cost across the passes, are featured. Gilded images and carved silver Buddha cases from Napal sell at cut prices alongside similar objects of superior workmanship from Eastern Tibet. Out in the street sit roadside vendors, their wares spread on blankets in front of them. From them you can buy rugs, donkey bells, tea bowls, padlocks, Indian matches, holy objects and bullets for almost any make of rifle.

There is no taxi problem in Lhasa; there is not a single cart. When you call on a friend or official you travel by horse, even if it is for only a few blocks. And always, if you are proper, you are accompanied by one or more attendants. You can judge the rank of an official by the number of horsemen he has with him and the splendor of their attire.

On several occasions, in Lhasa, I passed the father of the Dalai Lama, out for his daily ride. With his four red-hatted attendants mounted on splendid ponies, he could be spotted a long way off. As he approached, everyone along his route got off their mounts and inclined their heads, out of respect for his rank. He was himself richly gowned in a yellow silk robe partly covered by a cape of brilliant red. His yellow hat was aflame

Father and a brother of the Dalai Lama.

with red tassels.

The books say that Lhasa has a population of 50,000. It is hard to believe that there are more than 20,000 in the town itself. The neighboring monasteries, with their big population of monks, might add up to another 20,000.

Pending my meeting with the Dalai Lama, I did what any pilgrim to Lhasa is expected to do — I visited the holy places. I toured the dark recesses of the Great Temple. I went through the Potala. I climbed to the Temple of Medicine, where a few score monks are being schooled in the lore of herbs and incantations. I did the circuit of the Potala's outer walls over the Sacred Way,

Temple near Potala.
(Note: yak-hair curtains suspended from upper balcony.)

rodden deep by countless Tibetan pilgrims through the years.

The Great Temple is perhaps the holiest place in a coun-
ry full of holy places. Parts of it date back over a thousand
ears. Obscurely situated, in the heart of the crowded town, it
was easily identified by the numerous pilgrims prostrating themselves in front of its pillared entrance. A monk, carrying a one-
candlepower butter lamp, led me through cavernous passages
lined with cavelike openings. In these dark and musty grottoes
reposed hundreds of images of considerable antiquity. At the
entrance of each hung massive screens of hand-wrought iron
which at night are secured with intricate padlocks of jumbo
size. Many of the lamps and offertory vessels are of solid gold or
silver, and the images are in many cases studded with coral,
turquoise, jade and other semiprecious stones.

As a mark of respect for the founder of Buddhism, visitors
are expected to deposit a silk scarf at the feet of the famous
image of Jo Wo Rimpoche (Buddha as a prince), said to have
been brought to Lhasa more than 1,000 years ago by the
Chinese wife of an early Tibetan king. In the flickering half-light
of the butter lamps, the figure has a ghostly splendor, enhanced
by the glitter of gems and the fierce mien of the two sculptured
dragons which flanked it. Somewhere in the surrounding black-
ness, monks were beating drums and chanting prayers in voices
so low and guttural that they seemed to come from the bowels
of the earth.

The Great Temple is a veritable Shangri-la for mice. They
frolic around the statuary, nibble at the offerings of butter and
tsamba (barley flour) and seem oblivious to the worshipers. The
monks would not dream of harming them. In one cubicle, I

counted 20 of the saucy little rodents, running up, down and around a god's image.

The Potala, where I went next, was less impressive inside than out. The Dalai Lama lives here during the winter, but spends the warm season at his summer palace outside the town. The rooms of the Potala are for the most part small and dark, decorated with musty hangings and Buddhist images. But the tombs of the Dalai Lamas buried here are indeed striking monuments to the veneration in which these incarnations of the patron god, Chenrezi, were held by their subjects. Greatest of the Dalai Lamas were the Fifth and the Thirteenth (the latter died only a few years ago) and their tombs are therefore the biggest and the richest. All the tombs are in the dome-shaped pattern of a Buddhist chorten and are entirely covered with gold leaf. They range up to 60 feet in height. Each has its own golden roof, surmounting the flat top of the Potala. It is these that cause the huge building to glisten from afar.

The costly offerings of foreign governments and of devout Buddhists are arranged in front of the tombs or set into their surface. In a room surrounding the resting place of the Thirteenth Dalai Lama, the walls are covered with colorful murals done by a Tibetan artist and depicting the life and travels of that twice-exiled ruler. In India and China the Dalai Lama has made contact with such things as railway trains and steamships. The artist's conception of these foreign contraptions was interesting. The locomotive looked like a combination of Stephenson's "Rocket" and a Model-T Ford. The ship resembled Noah's ark under steam.

Everybody in Lhasa does the sacred walk around the

Potala at least once a year, some more often. For my limited sta-
mina, once was enough. It was a five-mile hike, done always in
a clockwise direction. Every day, pilgrims are to be seen making
the circuit, usually with prayer wheels in hand. The prayer
wheels are metal cylinders, stuffed with printed prayers, mounted and on a stick. To give effect to the prayers you simply twirl
the wheel. Most pilgrims also mumble prayers continuously
during the walk. The merit accumulated is considerable.

Following the Sacred Way, I first skirted a small stream.
Good Buddhists toss crumbs to the fish that it contains. The trail
continued, then, along a rocky slope where every foot of surface was covered with carvings of religious significance. Farther
on, there is a stone in which thousands of the faithful have worn
two deep grooves simply by rubbing their knees against it. It is
alleged to be a sure cure for rheumatism. I came upon a patch
of sand frequented by several hundred roosters. It is meritorious
to feed them. Back of the Potala I passed a colony of beggars,
living in shacks made entirely from the horns of sheep. To refuse
their plea for alms is to draw a curse. From here on, the Sacred
Way crossed open countryside and circled back into the town,
where dogs lay in great numbers also awaiting the offerings of
the devout.

The Grand Lama of Tibet — a boy of 9 — received us in
his throne room at the Jewel Park, outside Lhasa. I was one of
many who came to see him that morning, but nearly all the others were Tibetans who had come to seek his blessing. Also,
there were relatives of the Maharaja of Bhutan, a neighboring
Buddhist state. They were on a religious pilgrimage to Lhasa.

While waiting for the signal to enter, we sat on rugs outside the audience room and drank tea. Meanwhile, our gifts were sent in on trays carried by our servants. Mine were of a token nature, only, and consisted of a small sum of money and a plain silver bowl. But the money, in accordance with custom, had been converted into copper coins and wrapped in cotton bags, so that it made up in bulk what it lacked in value.

It took 20 coolies, on the other hand, to carry the numerous presents brought by the emissaries from Bhutan. Laid across their arms were bolts of colorfully patterned Bhutan cloth, rich embroideries, rolls of silk, trays of money, sacks of Bhutan rice and other articles of value.

The signal came from a priest official. We stepped into line and filed into the reception hall. It was a low-ceilinged room with numerous supporting pillars, decorated Tibetan fashion, with scrolls and silken hangings. On the right, nearly filling the room, more than 100 monks sat crosslegged on floor rugs. These were priest officials of the Tibetan government who are required every morning to attend the Dalai Lama's reception. They do not speak, but they drink gallons of Tibetan tea, served from huge silver containers.

At the far end of the aisle, the young Dalai Lama sat in the attitude of Buddha on an elevated seat. He was gowned in a maroon-colored robe, but scarves of white silk covered his crossed legs. At the Dalai Lama's right was the throne of the regent. The latter was absent that morning, but his robe of office, propped in his chair, denoted his spiritual presence.

The alert-eyed, rosy-cheeked boy on the pedestal gave me a smile of recognition (I had met him several years before, under very different circumstances, at a monastery in northwest-

Delegation with gifts for Dalai Lama entering Dalai Lama's throne room in Jewel Park, Lhasa.

ern China). Standing in front of him, I went through the customary ritual of greeting. I had brought with me a special kind of silk scarf, called "nang-tso," and used only for the Dalai Lama. This I unrolled and held across my two hands. In it, the attending lord chamberlain placed a symbol representing the world. I passed this to the boy Lama. Then, in quick succession, I passed on three other symbols representing the body, the speech and the mind. Finally the scarf itself was presented. Not a word was spoken.

I went through the same procedure at the empty throne of the regent, only in this case a scarf of lesser quality was employed. I retired then to a floor rug alongside the aisle and food offerings symbolic of welcome were brought to me. First came tea, then a heaping bowl of rice. The rice was not to be eaten but simply flicked with the fingers. A trayful of a sort of fried bread was also presented. This was to be taken home.

We sat for 15 minutes, watching a long line of Tibetan monks, officials and pilgrims pass down the aisle for the Dalai Lama's blessing. A giant monk kept the line moving with the efficiency of a Chicago traffic cop. The youthful priest-king touched each bobbing head as it passed under him, sometimes with his hands, more often with a tassel of vari-colored silk attached to a short handle. The kind of blessing granted depended on the rank and status of the recipient. The two-handed blessing was reserved for the highest officials and Lamas. Most officials and all monks were touched with only one hand. Everyone else, including all women, got the tassel.

The Dalai Lama handled his duties with remarkable smoothness, poise and self-possession. He must have blessed two or three hundred that morning, and it was not a big day. Many of the passing throng were pilgrims from remote regions of the country, among them long-haired herdsmen in sheep-skins. Some were so overawed at being in "The Presence" that they dared not look up. A few tossed coins at the foot of the throne as they filed by. They were given ringlets of silk to wear about their neck as proof that they had been blessed by their all-highest.

When the big monk bellowed an order of dismissal the crowd filed out through the intricately carved gateway of the courtyard entrance. They streamed down a long avenue lined with flowers and through the outer gate guarded by two stone

Dalai Lama, (Kumbum Monastery)
Before actually being named Dalai Lma.
At this time there were 3 candidates for "Discovery"

lions and members of the Dalai Lama's bodyguard. Large numbers of richly caparisoned mules and horses awaited their owners.

The Priest-King
and His Councilors

I venture to say that no ruler anywhere commands greater devotion from his people than the priest-king of Tibet. To all Tibetans, except perhaps for a few Christian converts on the outer fringes of the country, the Dalai Lama is of divine origin — the incarnation of the many-headed, many-armed patron deity of Tibet, Chenrezi.

The veneration in which he is held is indicated by the names which have been applied to him. He is the "Precious Protector," the "Precious Sovereign," "God's Vice-Regent on Earth," the "All-Knowing Presence." Most often he is referred to as "The Presence."

The only Tibetan dignitary who approaches the Dalai Lama in spiritual importance is the Panchen Lama. The last Panchen Lama died in 1937 and his successor has not yet been found. Reports that a boy in west China has been designated as the new Panchen Lama are flatly denied in Lhasa, where I was told that three boys are still under consideration. In past years, rivalry between Tashi Lhunpo, the seat of the Panchen Lama, and Lhasa, the seat of the Dalai Lama, has sometimes caused

Photo taken by Steele in 1939 of the Dalai Lama and several monks,
about the time when the child was being examined for supernatural signs
as proof of his claim to the throne of Tibet. Shortly after this picture was
taken he was escorted to Lhasa and installed on the gilded throne. Note
his humble appearance compared with his later splendor. He was the son
of a wretchedly poor peasant living in the vicinity of Kumbum Monastery.
He was then only 4 years old, but he was already beginning to show
remarkable qualities. Steele was probably the first foreigner he had seen,
yet he was quite unabashed and showed a dignity far beyond his years.

trouble in Tibetan politics.

Tibetans believe that when a Dalai Lama dies the soul enters the body of a child. The present boy-ruler, son of a humble peasant, is the fourteenth Dalai Lama. Some Dalai Lamas have been great, some mediocre. At least four died young under mysterious circumstances. Presumably they were poisoned. Even today, it is customary for tea and food to be tasted by an attendant before it is set before the Dalai Lama.

As a priest-king, the Dalai Lama can never marry. Only one of his predecessors is known to have veered from the rule of celibacy. He is one of those who died young.

The thirteenth Dalai Lama lived to be 57 and died in 1933. The present incarnation was born two years later on a little farm near Kumbum Monastery, close to the Chinese border town of Sining. He was not discovered and "recognized," however, until he was 4 years old.

In their search for the new Dalai Lama, the Tibetan authorities first consulted their gods as to the probable direction in which he would be found. The state oracle, in a trance, pointed east. The body of the late Dalai Lama, lying in state in the Potala, is alleged to have turned twice toward the east. A strange fungus appeared suddenly on the east side of his tomb. It was still there, enclosed in glass, when I visited the tomb.

In search of further signs, the regent made a pilgrimage to a sacred lake 10 days out of Lhasa. In its rippling waters he is said to have seen the reflection of three letters of the Tibetan alphabet and of a three-storied, golden-roofed temple. Wise men decided that one of the letters, "Ah," stood for the Amdo district in northeastern Tibet. The three-storied temple undoubtedly represented a temple of like appearance at Kumbum Monastery in Amdo. It happened that the temple was named after the Buddhist saint Ka-ma-pa, which accounted for the other two letters, "Kah" and "Mah."

With the search thus narrowed, Lhasa sent a delegation of high monks to select the true incarnation from one of three promising candidates in the Kumbum area. It did not take long. At the humble home of a farmer, Chog Chu Tsering, they found a 4-year-old boy who showed all the supernatural manifestations. The boy is reputed to have unerringly selected two necklaces and a cane belonging to the late Dalai Lama from a group of such articles laid before him. He ignored the imitations. On his body were found three markings indicative of his connection with the god Chenrezi. There were other signs, too, to clinch the identification.

The boy could not be brought to Lhasa—a two-month journey—until a goodly sum had been paid to the Chinese governor of the border region. It was not until late in 1939 that he was installed on his throne in Lhasa. The British, the Chinese and the little states of Nepal, Bhutan and Sikkim sent delegations with gifts. The British present, for instance, included a brick of gold, 10 bags of silver, three rifles, six rolls of broadcloth, a gold watch, three stoves, a garden hammock, a music box and an English saddle.

Since coming to Lhasa, the boy has learned to read, write and speak Tibetan and is fast forgetting his native Chinese dialect.

Almost his only associates are monks and lamas and the members of his own family. His day is a full one. He is up at dawn, says his prayers and for the next hour or so practices handwriting. At 9 he holds his daily reception, blessing all who come before him. The rest of the morning is devoted to reading the Buddhist classics. He commits much to memory. After the noon interval, the child goes to work again on his calligraphy and in midafternoon resumes his study of the holy books. There is time for play, then, with his brothers. He is in bed by 9:00, but not before he has chanted lengthy prayers.

Those closest to him are probably his mother, who is well liked in Lhasa, and the lord chamberlain, a monk of the old school but of fine appearance, gentle manner and considerable learning.

Aristocrats and priests share the task of ruling Tibet, but the priests hold the upper hand. Every third man in Tibet is a monk. Every family in Tibet has one or more of its members in the priesthood. The monks are from the people and are close to them.

The nobility is powerful, too, but in a different way. It is a class of wealthy landlords, with far-reaching powers over their tenants. It is an exclusive class which has intermarried for generations and seldom admits people of lower status to its ranks. The social void between the aristocracy and the common people is very wide. The social system of Tibet is a close parallel to the feudal structure of the middle ages in Europe. Yet it seems to work. The people accept their lowly place. There are few stirrings of nationalism as yet in Buddhist Tibet.

The Dalai Lama is all-powerful. He is the spiritual leader of the country and, when he comes of age, in another eight years, he will assume full temporal leadership, too. His authority will then be absolute in all things. None dare challenge him openly, for in the people's eyes he rules under a mandate from heaven.

Pending the emergence of the Dalai Lama from boyhood, the final authority in matters of government is the regent. He is an incarnation lama, 71 years old, and is a paragon of conservatism. When I met him at his residence at the Tak-tra Monastery, outside Lhasa, he sat with quiet dignity on an elevated seat befitting his rank and talked in a low, almost inaudible voice — a mark of culture and learning in Tibet.

Most of the real work of government, however, is done by a cabinet of four men called the Kashag. They are appointees of the regent and work closely with him. None of the Kashag's decisions can take effect until the regent has approved them. Three of the cabinet members are of the nobility, but the fourth, a high lama, has seniority. Both the regent and his Kashag are sensitive to the wishes of the Tibetan priesthood. Especially influential are the three great monasteries in the vicinity of Lhasa—Drepung, Sera and Ganden. History has shown more than once what a powerful force these monk cities, with a total population of 20,000, can become when aroused to action. They can be militant, on occasion. And they fear nobody except the Dalai Lama.

I met the members of the Kashag as a group and in their homes. They excelled in courtly courtesy. We talked about America, about the war, about airplanes. They wanted American friendship but they did not want the American style of civilization. Their conservatism came out when I asked whether Tibet, at some future time, might wish to embrace some of the

The Dalai Lama

ways of the West. They agreed that that would depend on the
wishes of the Dalai Lama when he comes of age but that in the
meantime Tibet would stay as it is.

People who want change are not popular in Tibet today

The Dalai Lama

and they don't last long in important official positions.

Although the regent and the Kashag hold most of the governmental power, they are subject to certain checks. There is a body, for instance, called the National Assembly which has the authority (seldom exercised) to vote out a regent who does not satisfy them. This is not an elected assembly as the name might imply, but is composed simply of several hundred of the more important government officials. It is assembled on invitation from the regent and the Kashag when there are issues of special urgency before the government. It is a stronghold of priestly influence.

One of the most interesting and able groups of men I met in Lhasa was the so-called "Monk Cabinet," composed of the four priests who supervise the general affairs of all the monasteries in Tibet and control the training and appointment of priest officials in the government. As spokesmen for the powerful priesthood, their influence is great. Talking to these maroon-robed clerics over a tea table at the Dalai Lama's palace, I was impressed by their shrewd though ultraconservative outlook on Tibetan affairs.

A unique feature of the Tibetan government is that half the government posts are held by laymen and half by monks. Lay officials are recruited entirely from sons of officials (the aristocracy). Their government pay is small but most of them are independently wealthy. They are permitted to make what they can on the side, and the opportunities are numerous. The monk officials, on the other hand, come from the rank and file of the priesthood, whose high birth confers its privileges. This is the democratic side of a system which is otherwise autocratic. The

Monk Cabinet

Dalai Lama is nearly always a boy of humble birth.

Government revenues come mostly from taxes and donations, nearly always in the form of farm products. But the big
estates of the monasteries are free from taxation.

Religion always gets the breaks in this country.

The only wheeled thing I saw during two months in Tibet
was a bicycle owned by a messenger in the British mission at
Lhasa. And that was such a curiosity that people would stop to
stare at it as it went by. Lhasa-controlled Tibet has no automobiles in circulation, although two cars owned by the progres-
sively-minded thirteenth Dala Lama are said to be accumulating
rust and dust somewhere on the palace grounds. They have not
given a gasp for 10 years and will probably never run again.

"The Mail Goes Through", even if it is only by foot. This is a Tibetan mail runner, on the trail to Lhasa, skirting the shore of the Yamdrok Lake. He carries a short spear with bells on it, as a mark of identification. The mail is on his back. He will run five miles and then turn over his load to another, who will take up the chase.

These museum pieces were brought across the Himalayas in sections, on the backs of men and animals.

Some 20 years ago, the British brought a light car, by the same means, into southern Tibet, hoping to speed up their mail service to Gyantse. But the fire-spitting horseless carriage so panicked the livestock along the way that it had to be withdrawn from service. Besides, the monks were against it.

As far as I know, these are the only automobiles that ever got into central Tibet. Their lives were short.

More recently an effort was made to introduce motorcycles in Lhasa. A few sons of the aristocracy, who had been to India and seen the pace at which the outer world lives, thought that the motorcycles would be useful and recreational. Some half dozen of the machines reached the Tibetan capitol. But not all of them saw service. Before the last of them could be unpacked, the government issued an official ban. It was held that they frightened animals, disturbed the tranquility of the holy city and were frowned upon by the gods.

That was two years ago. About the same time, a prohibition was issued against foreign style dress and the playing of English football. The British had innocently introduced the game into Lhasa and it was becoming popular. One day, during a match, a fierce hailstorm descended on the Lhasa region, seriously damaging crops. This was interpreted as a sign of the wrath of the gods. No football has been played since.

The Tibetans, in short, with a few exceptions, are not interested in the ways of the outside world. The only type of progress that the average Tibetan is concerned with is his progress toward a higher plane of existence in his next incarnation. This requires good living, meditation and prayer in this life. It does not require airplanes, automobiles, moving pictures or machines. Tibetans are mighty pleased to be out of the war and they think their seclusion and religion have something to do with it. One view is that we in America and Europe are simply paying the price of offending the gods.

Airplanes would speed up travel enormously in Tibet. Trips which now take weeks or months could be accomplished in a few hours. Yet the only plane that ever came down in central Tibet was the one that crashed, near Lhasa last winter while off-course in a flight from China to India. The five Yanks in the big four-engined transport managed to bail out in the nick of time and made their way overland to India with Chinese, British and Tibetan assistance. Tibetans had been told by their priests that no foreign plane could invade the sacred sky over Lhasa and survive.

Tibet is almost a country without machinery. There is a small power plant in Lhasa but it supplies only a few buildings and with very feeble light. One of the few modern touches in the vicinity of Lhasa is a steel bridge, of three spans, across a small river west of the town. It was built at the cost of tremendous efforts with girders carried from India by battalions of porters. It took three years to complete. Today it is a useful but incongruous feature of the Tibetan landscape. In Lhasa I met the former cabinet member, Tsarong, who built the bridge. A man of forward-looking views, he is one of the outstanding Tibetans that I have met. He is at present in retirement.

Tibet has its own currency and its own postal system, but the postal routes are few. Runners, jogging along the trail in five- mile relays, carry the mail from Lhasa to Gyantse, where there is a link with the British-managed pony express to India and the outside world. The runners carry short spears with bells attached, as a symbol of their identity. The sole telegraph line in Tibet runs from the Indian border to Lhasa, along the main trade route. It consists of one wire. The British operate it as far as

Gyantse, the Tibetans from there to the capital.

There are wireless sets in Tibet, but no broadcasting station. Tibet has no newspapers. When I asked an official why, his reply was "Nothing ever happens in this country."

"On The Roof of the World"

I met all kinds of people in Lhasa but few who were closer to the gods than the Nechung Oracle, chief prophet for the Tibetan government. At least once a month, and sometimes more often, this state oracle goes into a trance. In that condition he becomes the spokesman for the deity which is supposed to have entered his body. His predictions are thus clothed with special significance.

The oracle prepares himself for a trance with a day or two of frequent bathing and meditation. On the appointed day he dons special clothes and headdress and takes his seat on a throne. On his front hangs a shiny metal disc. An attendant monk begins chanting, the oracle closes his eyes and appears to drift into unconsciousness. He trembles violently and often rises to his feet and does a dance. The audience gathers around to ask questions, any questions, dealing with the future. The oracle seems to lose control of himself. Sometimes he collapses, sometimes reels into the arms of the spectators. On recovering consciousness, he professes to recollect nothing of what he has said. It takes him two or three days to get over the exhaustion of the ordeal.

The state oracle of Tibet with A.T. Steele. The oracle occasionally goes into trance and in that state makes predictions, but in this picture he is at ease.

I did not see the Nechung Oracle in a trance, but I met him under less exciting circumstances at his temple, about an hour's horseback ride out of Lhasa. Dressed in flowing yellow silk of a Chinese pattern, he received me in a little room thickly hung with Buddhist paintings. He proved to be a man of keen wit and amiability. I was questioned about the United States. He seemed skeptical, however, when I told him that America could be reached by traveling either in a westerly or easterly direction. Most Tibetans believe that the world is flat.

There are many holy men in Tibet claiming powers of prophecy, but the Nechung Oracle outranks them all. His forecasts are accepted with the utmost respect. Not all oracles make good. Those whose prognostications fail to hold up are quickly discredited as false prophets.

A mile or so up the hill from the oracle's home lies Drepung Monastery, the biggest monastery in the world. Nestling in a rocky ravine, its closely bunched cluster of whitewashed buildings shelters 10,000 monks. I rode up to see it. Two red-robed proctors, carrying symbolic bronze shafts of authority, led the way up the narrow, hillside streets, shouting as they walked: "Stand clear! Stand clear!" The shouted injunction was well heeded by the priestly inhabitants. Few showed their faces, although a number, unable to curb their curiosity, peeked at us from windows and rooftops. We walked, thus, through ghostly streets, to the topmost building in the monastery where three of the abbots welcomed us with tea and ceremonial rice. They were men stooped with years of obeisance and prayer, but there was homely wisdom in their faces. They showed us through the huge, semi-darkened halls lined with silk-clad

Monks answering call to prayer in alleyway of Drepung Monastery which at the time (1944) was thought to be the largest monastery in the world (population 10,000).

images and peopled with a few chanting monks. In the kitchen, tea was being prepared for the priests in metal caldrons 10 feet across.

Life in Lhasa is not all prayer. There is gaiety, too. Lhasa parties make up for the absence of movies, newspapers and other diversions to which the Western world is accustomed. The latest news and gossip is quickly spread by word of mouth. The barley beer flows freely, and light though it is, it has a telling effect in the end; for the parties last most of the day. In the park where my house was situated, Tibetan families often pitched their fanciest tents and gave all-day parties. My back yard became an archery court. Lhasa dandies, gleaming with turquoise, coral and silver, shot whistling arrows at the large bull's-eye.

One day a monk visited me, carrying a white scarf and an invitation from the regent to a party at his home, 10 miles from town. I rode out on horseback with my guides, reaching the hillside house at about 10 in the morning. The British guests arrived at about the same time, having halted about a mile out to divest themselves of the extra pants which they had worn to protect their party clothing. It was a three-day party, and this was the second day. In a big courtyard, under a canvas awning, a company of masked and painted Tibetan troupers were putting on a kind of operetta which went on without a break throughout the day. Officials and monks sat according to rank in three tiers of balconies, with the regent in the uppermost. Several hundred peasants formed a dense ring on the ground around the arena. Two monks 7 feet tall watched over them with horsewhips, occasionally taking a swipe at over-eager spectators.

Tea came to us frequently during the performance, and in late morning and midafternoon we were served excellent meals, including such hard-to-get delicacies as shark fins and seaweed. As every new performer entered, he prostrated himself before the balcony occupied by the regent. At the end of the show, a line of porters entered the arena bearing presents from the regent to the actors. Not till sundown were we back in Lhasa.

As an unsolved international puzzle, the hermit kingdom of Tibet poses complexities and dangers which the peacemakers of the world will be unable to ignore when the time comes for the reshaping of Asia. The countries most directly concerned are China and Britain. But America too, with its professed concern for the rights of minority peoples, is an interested spectator. Russia, in Czarist days, strove for a political foothold in Tibet, but has shown little interest since the Bolshevik revolution. The proximity of Tibet and the Soviet Union, however, makes one wonder whether the Russian unconcern is permanent.

The nub of the situation is this: Since Lhasa expelled the shadowy authority of China during the Chinese revolution 32 years ago, the Tibetans have enjoyed more or less complete self-rule. There is no question the majority want to stay that way. It is quite possible that they would consent to a nominal Chinese suzerainty, but only at the price of real internal autonomy and a fixed frontier. Tibet's trouble is that she is militarily weak. She cannot be sure of her future until her powerful neighbors have come to an understanding. This has not been forthcoming. The British and the Chinese, for instance, hold conflicting views. The Tibetan question ranks with the Hong Kong

(Kowloon) question as one of the two major points of difference between Britain and China.

For the British, Tibet's huge mountainous land mass is a valuable buffer against encroachment on India from the north. For 1,300 miles, Tibet borders on the northern fringe of the Indian subcontinent, but as long as Tibet remains an autonomous void the danger of foreign encroachment from that side is negligible. Should other powers gain a military hold on Tibet, however, India's defense problem would be greatly complicated, according to the British view. It might be necessary to station bigger forces along the Himalayan frontier. There would be danger, too, of political penetration in the Indian border states. One or two of these states once had loose connections with China.

British military penetration in Tibet is confined to a 150-mile stretch of trail between India and Gyantse on the main trade route. Here the British maintain fewer than 100 Indian troops, as an escort for the British trade agencies. The mail service and telephone line to Gyantse are also under British control, but Lhasa's administrative authority is unaffected.

These British rights were fruits of the Younghusband expedition in 1903-4. Col. Younghusband, with a few thousand troops, fought his way to Lhasa, but later withdrew. A treaty signed then provided for establishment of British trade agencies in three towns of western and southern Tibet and for their protection. The Younghusband expedition was precipitated by fear that the Russians were about to gain a political grip on Tibet.

Although for many years the British have had direct dealings with the Lhasa government, they have stood ready to recognize China's theoretical suzerainty. The British government takes the line that Chinese suzerainty can be fully admitted if Tibet is granted full autonomy.

The Chinese view on Tibet begins with the premise that Tibet is historically, culturally and geographically a part of China. The Chinese are unhappy over the partiality of certain Lhasa officials toward the British and are critical of the British foothold — small though it is — on the India-Gyantse trade route. Shen Chung-lien, the smart, Harvard-educated Chinese delegate in Lhasa, told me that China is prepared to recognize Tibet's domestic autonomy but insists that the country's foreign affairs should be handled through the Chinese government. He contended that the real issue is not between China and Tibet but between China and Britain.

What worries the Tibetans (and the British) is just what the Chinese mean by autonomy.

In Lhasa, I got the impression that the British had many friends among the officials, but the latter were extremely discreet in their views. They seem to feel that the most they could hope for in case of a crisis with China is diplomatic assistance. Thus, they are doing nothing to antagonize the Chinese.

When President Roosevelt sent an autographed portrait of himself and a letter of greeting to the Dalai Lama last year, he raised an issue which has not yet been clarified. Did this gesture constitute a tacit recognition by the American executive of Tibet's autonomous position?

The picture and the message were carried to Lhasa by two American Army officers making an inspection trip of the trans-Tibetan caravan route to China. They also bore numerous and valuable gifts of their own for Tibetan officials. The visit undoubtedly raised hopes among some Tibetans that the United States was interested in their problems and might become an influence in helping them to preserve their autonomy.

Whether these hopes are justified is by no means clear, Washington has not spoken.

Tibetans believe that they have a strong racial and historical basis for their claims to self-rule, within or without the Chinese framework. The three to five million Tibetans (nobody is quite sure how many there are) who live up here on the roof of the world are of Mongoloid roots but differ from the Chinese in many ways. They speak and write a language which has little resemblance to the Chinese; it is closer to the Burmese. Culturally, they have borrowed more from the Chinese than from any other people, although they owe much to India.

Historically, Chinese-Tibetan relations date back at least 1,200 years, and probably much longer. But it was not until the 18th century that the Chinese managed to assert real authority in Lhasa. From then on, the Chinese-Tibetan connection went through numerous ups and downs until at last the Chinese revolution gave the Tibetans an opportunity to throw off the last traces of Chinese control, which by that time had grown very weak. The Chinese amban and his troops were driven from the country. Since then, the Chinese have been too deeply involved in domestic travail and in their war with Japan to reassert their lost authority in Lhasa. Occasional incursions have enabled the Chinese, however, to absorb a wide zone in populous eastern Tibet. The very indefinite and still unrecognized boundary between Chungking and Lhasa administration follows roughly the line of the Upper Yangtze.

There are really two Tibets. The first is the territory controlled by the Tibetan government with an area of about half a million square miles. The second is the territory inhabited largely by people of Tibetan race. The second includes all the first plus an outer fringe, about a third as big, not under Lhasa's administration.

The spiritual influence of Lhasa goes much farther. In Inner Mongolia, Chinese Turkestan and parts of India there are several million Buddhists who recognize the Dalai Lama as their spiritual leader. That is another potent reason why China and Britain are eager for Lhasa's friendship.

The Tibetan army numbers scarcely 5,000 men, and they are lacking in training and equipment. Monastic influences in Tibet are traditionally opposed to a strong army, not only for religious reasons but because of the fear that it might be used to curb their power. Just the same, when the country is threatened with invasion, the monks usually join in the fight. Monks in arms are called the "Golden Army."

Tibet relies mainly for protection on the successive ranges of mountains which surround the heart of the country. It was not until an American transport plane crashed near Lhasa that many Tibetans realized that their capital could even be reached by air. Now they realize that their mighty peaks and high passes would be no bar to air-borne landings.

Although Tibet is an arena of keen Anglo-Chinese rivalry, Tibetans want no trouble with their neighbors. What bothers them a little is the possibility that a victorious and nationalist China may, after the war, turn its attention to Tibet and force a

A Tibetan soldier dressed up for review.

showdown on outstanding issues. For several years the Chinese have been pushing roads into eastern Tibet, and they have air-dromes near the Tibetan frontier.

All parties concerned in the Tibetan problem want an early understanding but agreement may be difficult. Views have recently been exchanged in Lhasa between Sir Basil Gould, the British representative, and Shen Chung-lien, the Chinese dele-gate. The talks have been of a wholly informal nature and yet give no particular cause for optimism. But both are men of tact and understanding who seem to be able to get along with the Tibetans.

Last Days in 'Shangri-la'

There are no Americans in Lhasa-controlled Tibet and Europeans are so scarce that they are still a curiosity. In almost any Tibetan town, a freshly arrived white man, wearing the habitat of his country, will attract as big a crowd of onlookers as would a head-hunter from the Burma jungle set down suddenly at 42nd and Broadway. We are funny looking. We have big noses. Our faces are red, our jowls are hairy, we wear silly clothes. Put yourself into a Tibetan's boots and you will understand.

Virtually the only Christian missionaries in Tibet are those working in border regions outside Lhasa's control. Tibetan Buddhists are extremely resistant to conversion. Yet they are not intolerant. Although they do not welcome missionaries they raise no objections to the existence of two small Mohammedan mosques in Lhasa, where there is a considerable colony of Chinese and Ladakhi (northwestern India) Muslims.

The white population of Lhasa is very small. It consists, normally, of the British diplomatic representative and his wife, a British radio operator and a British schoolteacher. Permits for foreigners to visit Lhasa are seldom granted and the length of stay is usually limited. Lhasa has relaxed its prohibitions slightly in recent years but it is still pretty much of a forbidden city.

There are several hundred Nepalese and Ladakhi traders in Lhasa and more than 2,000 Chinese. Many of the Chinese have married Tibetans and some — of the second and third generation — are unable to speak the language of their Chinese ancestors.

Except for little Nepal and still smaller Bhutan, China and British India are the only countries that have diplomatic missions in Lhasa. Their status is paradoxical. The Chinese mission goes under the name of the Tibet Office of the Tibetan and Mongolian Affairs Commission of the Chinese Government, which implies some degree of Chinese authority. The Tibetans, for their part, prefer to call the Chinese representative a "special delegate." The British mission is a "temporary" one but it has been there since 1937 and Tibetan officials seem to wish it to stay on.

When the Chinese re-established direct negotiation with Lhasa in 1934, after a lengthy breach, they brought a wireless station with them. The British followed up with one of their own in 1937. Tibetans, being without radio facilities, had access to either of them. Now the Lhasa government is installing equipment of its own but it will be used only for communication with outposts within the country. The equipment is a gift from the United States.

Both the British and the Chinese maintain small hospitals in Lhasa where Tibetans can come for free treatment if their own herbal concoctions fail them. A few come despite a mild popular prejudice against foreign medicine. Venereal disease is common but the scourge most feared is smallpox. Vaccination is now common practice, even for the Dalai Lama.

Schools in Tibet are chiefly under monastic influence and are few. Reading and writing are almost the only subjects taught and the reading is mainly religious. Tibetans have little conception of the history or geography of the rest of the world. To most of them the United States is just a big, vague country across an ocean. Some, in the backwoods, have never heard of it. Nobody I spoke to in Lhasa knew of any Tibetans who had been to America, although a few officials told me, politely, that they would like to go there.

Remarkably few Tibetans have been abroad. With the priesthood in the ascendency the influence of these few is, for the present, small. Years ago four Tibetan boys were sent to England for technical training. Two are still living. A number of the Tibetan aristocracy have been to India to visit the holy seats of Buddhism and to get their first view of railway trains, automobiles, factories and tenements. There are probably a few among them who would favor the introduction of some Occidental innovations. But they know that this is not the time to advance their views. Even mining is forbidden in Tibet. It would displease the deities to rob the earth of its wealth. But religion is not the only reason for Tibet's aversion to change. Tibetan leaders know that such things as railways and mining concessions often bring foreign pressure and foreign armies.

Fabulous Shangri-la is better known in the United States than in Tibet. Tibetans have never heard of it. But they have their own conception of a mythical foreign land. It is called Shambala, and it is supposed to lie somewhere north of Tibet, which only goes to prove that you can never quite catch up with a rainbow.

The nearest thing to the Hollywood conception of Shangri-la that I encountered in Tibet was in Lhasa's Jewel Park, site of the summer palace of the Dalai Lama. Here is a place of charm and beauty, where the boy-pope lives an existence of prayer and study surrounded by priestly tutors and advisors.

I was struck with this on my second meeting with the Dalai Lama, in the inner compound of Jewel Park. The inner walls were well guarded. Two dogs as big as small bears, and equally as shaggy, leaped from their kennels at each side of the entrance, to give us a noisy greeting. I was relieved to see that they were securely chained.

Inside the enclosure was a small lake, surrounded by aspens and gnarled willows. We crossed a foot-bridge to a tiny island in the middle of the pond. Here, on the balcony of a many-columned pavilion, sat the youthful Dalai Lama, attended by devoted priest-followers. His raised throne was set amid a mass of potted chrysanthemums and was flanked, at each end of the balcony, by a magnificent pair of scowling bronze lions — the gift, long ago, of some Chinese emperor.

Again, no words were spoken by the boy, but he submitted willingly, and with amusement, to the taking of photographs.

My two weeks in Lhasa were now almost at an end. Officials came to my cottage to return the calls I had made on them. Some simply sent messengers with the symbolic white scarves and usually a present of small rugs or handwoven wool cloth. The most unexpected callers were a group of the Tibetan

The Dalai Lama on an outdoor throne in the inner compound of his summer palace. The man on the left is Lord Chamberlain.

equivalent of undertakers. These are the men who break up the bodies of the dead and feed them to the vultures. It was explained that they were accustomed to receiving tips from foreign visitors.

Before leaving Lhasa I paid a visit to the Dalai Lama's father at his new house next to the Potala. He looked much like a Chinese mandarin of the old school in his silken robes and his tasseled, conical hat. A man of humble origin, he has been lifted from poverty to wealth and position beyond his dreams by the lucky chance of his son's elevation to the throne of Tibet. By custom, he has been made a "kung", or duke, and has been granted large estates befitting his title.

I took a last look at the bazaar and tried to snap pictures of its picturesque crowds. But the moment my camera was pointed, heads turned in the other direction and some of the vendors tried to hide themselves with their umbrellas. Several protested that the camera would rob them of their souls and cause their death. A few coins usually changed their views. Some contended that the danger would be neutralized if they could have copies of their photograph.

In Lhasa, as elsewhere in Tibet, I was swamped with tea. Tibetan tea is really a rich and nourishing soup. Its base is a kind of brick tea from China, but it contains also milk, butter, soda, salt and barley flour. A Tibetan kills time with a cup of tea as some of us kill time with a cigarette or a cigar. Smoking is forbidden in Lhasa, though a few indulge, in the privacy of their homes. Sniffing snuff is a popular addiction.

On the appointed day of departure, I slipped out of Lhasa in a boat — not a steamboat, or even a motorboat — for such conveniences are unknown — but in a yak-skin coracle. It was an all-day ride down the Kyi River to its junction with the Brahmaputra, but from there on, the journey was by horse. By double-staging, it was possible to shorten the return trip to India by a week.

It seemed strange to get back to a world of railways and automobiles. Even the midget, 1892-model locomotive on the train to Siliguri looked like a streamlined mechanical marvel. It seemed stranger still to get back to a world at war. Probably no country in the world is more remote from the war and less concerned with it than Tibet.

Tibetan Prayer Flag

AND THEN
THERE IS NOW

The Tragedy of Tibet

by Archibald T. Steele and Beatrice Baker

World maps generally show Tibet as a part of China, and now it is so recognized. But in the 1940s, Tibet was a separate nation governed by the Dalai Lama, a Shangri-la of peace and harmony.

During the summer of 1950, the Dalai Lama, then 15, and his advisors received a report that Chinese soldiers raided a Tibetan post, causing the death of the responsible officer. This was grave news indeed. The previous Autumn there had been cross-border invasions by Chinese communists, who stated their intention of liberating Tibet from the hand of imperialist aggressors. This was despite the fact that all Chinese officials living in Lhasa had been expelled in 1949.

To the Dalai Lama, it looked as if the Chinese were making good their threat and Tibet was in grave danger. The Tibetan army mustered no more than 8,500 officers and men, no match for the recently victorious Peoples Liberation Army (PLA) of the Chinese Cultural Revolution, inspired and directed by Chairman Mao Tse Tung.

Two months later in October their worst fears were fulfilled. Reports on Chinese radio announced that on the anniversary of the communists coming to power in China, an army of 80,000 soldiers of the PLA had crossed the Drichu River east of Chambo, the capital of Kahm. The "Peaceful Liberation" of Tibet had begun.

The ax had fallen, and soon, the city of Lhasa must fall.

Roving mobs swept the country of Tibet, leaving a trail of destruction, pillage and carnage in their wake. In some areas they met with fierce resistance. But no matter how large or how well prepared the Tibetan army had been, the Chinese population was more than a hundred times larger than the Tibetan.

The Chinese lost large numbers of men in their conquest of Tibet. They suffered great casualties from difficulties of supply on the one hand and the harsh climate on the other. Many died from starvation; others succumbed to altitude sickness, which has always plagued, and sometimes actually killed, foreigners in Tibet. (I can attest to the seriousness of this malady.)

This threat to the freedom of Tibet did not go unnoticed in the world. The Indian government, supported by the British government, protested to the People's Republic of China and stated that the invasion was not in the interests of peace. On November 7, 1950, the Kashag, the Tibetan four-man cabinet, and the government, appealed to the United Nations Organization to intercede on Tibet's behalf. Sadly, Tibet, following her policy of peaceful isolation, had never sought to become a member of the United Nations, so nothing came of this effort.

As winter drew on and the news got worse, people began to advocate giving the Dalai Lama his majority and full temporal power two years early. The question was put to the oracle

during a very tense ritual, at the end of which the Kuten, totter-
ing under the weight of his 75-pound, huge ceremonial headdress, came over to where the Dalai Lama sat and laid a Kata, a
white silk offering scarf, on the Dalai Lama's lap, intoning the
words "thu-la bap," "His time has come." The Oracle, Doye
Drakden, had spoken.

Number One Tutor Tathag Rinpoche (teacher) at once
prepared to retire as regent, though he wanted to remain as the
Senior Tutor. It remained only for the state astrologers to select
November 17, 1950, as the most auspicious day for enthronement before the end of the year.

A short time before the Dalai Lama's investiture, his eldest
brother, 18 years his senior, arrived. It was evident he had suffered greatly. Amdo, the province where both brothers were
born and in which the famous monastery Kumbum is situated,
lies close to China. It had quickly fallen under control of the
communists.

The Dalai Lama's brother, Taktsu Rinpoche (teacher), the
abbot of Kumbum Monastery, had difficulty telling his story.
Once Amdo was "liberated," restrictions were immediately put
on the activities of the monks and he, himself, was kept a prisoner within his monastery. His Chinese "liberators" endeavored
to indoctrinate him in the new, communist way of thinking.
They devised a plan whereby they would set him free to go to
Lhasa if he would undertake to persuade the Dalai Lama to
accept Chinese rule. If the Dalai Lama were to resist, his brother, an abbot, was to kill him.

It was a strange proposal. The idea of killing any living
creature is anathema to Buddhists. The suggestion that Taktsu

Rinpoche might actually assassinate the Dalai Lama for personal gain showed how little understanding the Chinese had of Tibetan character

For a year, the Dalai Lama's brother watched his community destroyed by the Chinese, gradually concluding that he must escape to Lhasa to warn the Dalai Lama and the government of what lay in store for Tibet if the Chinese conquered the country. The way to escape was to agree to do their bidding.

The young boy, the Dalai Lama, was shocked as his brother revealed the plot. Until that moment, the young ruler had almost no knowledge of the Chinese, and of communists he was entirely ignorant, although he was aware that they had been causing terrible hardships for the people of Mongolia. His brother's revelations made him realize that the communists were not only non-religious, but were actually opposed to the practice of religion.

The Dalai Lama became very frightened as his brother told of his fears. Taktsu Rinpoche was convinced that only foreign support could help Tibet resist the communists by force of arms.

The Buddha forbade killing, but had indicated that under certain circumstances, it could be justified. And to Taktsu Rinpoche, the present problems justified it.

Taktsu Rinpoche volunteered to renounce his monastic vows, disrobe and go abroad as an emissary for Tibet, confident that the Americans would support the idea of a free Tibet.

He urged the Dalai Lama to leave Lhasa; the danger was great, he warned. Others had voiced the same concern, but the Dalai Lama resisted the advice.

The Dalai Lama had two more meetings with his brother, but could not persuade him to change his mind. His brother's terrible experiences of the past year had convinced him that there was no other way. The Dalai Lama did not dwell on the matter as he had preoccupations of his own — his enthronement ceremony was only a few days away.

In his memoirs, the Dalai Lama describes the enthronement ceremony in colorful, amusing language. He found the proceedings long and tiring. And at the close, he found himself the undisputed leader of six million people facing the threat of a full-scale war. He was still only 15 years old. It was an impossible situation to be in.

Taktsu Rinpoche had discussions with various members of the government before leaving the capitol. It was decided that delegations be sent to America, Great Britain, and Napal in the hope of persuading these countries to intervene on Tibet's behalf. These missions left towards the end of the year.

Soon the Chinese were consolidating their forces in the east. With this new threat, it was decided that the Dalai Lama as well as the most senior members of government should move to southern Tibet. That way, if the situation continued to deteriorate, it would be possible for the Dalai Lama to seek exile across the border with India. Two senior officers were to remain in Lhasa in an acting capacity; the Dalai Lama would take the seals of state with him.

Preparations for the move were made secretly to avoid widespread panic. Some preparation was unknown even to the Dalai Lama. He was furious when he found that fifty or sixty strong boxes of treasure, mostly gold biscuits and silver bars from the vaults at the Potala, had been sent ahead with several baggage trains. The decision was that of Kenrup Tenzin, the former master of the robes, who had recently been promoted to Chiky ab Kempo. The Dalai Lama felt he was being treated as a child and his pride was wounded that he had not been consulted about such an important decision

For the Dalai Lama, the time of departure was a mixture of anxiety and anticipation. He was happy at the prospect of traveling and sad at the prospect of abandoning his people. He traveled dressed as a layman, which pleased him as he could see more of the country and observe his people.

They left Lhasa in the middle of the night, with the final destination was Droma, 200 miles distant. The entourage made an impressive column of at least 200 people, of which 50 were high officials, and a similar number of pack animals. They reached Gyantse (Tibet's fourth largest city) after almost a week of travel, arriving at Droma in January 1951 after a journey of almost a fortnight.

The Dalai Lama was pleased to again meet with his eldest brother, Taktsu Rinpoche, who had arrived earlier on his way to India. But Taktsu Rinpoche had received bad news of the delegations sent abroad before the Dalai Lama left Lhasa. Only one, the one to Napal, had reached its destination. Each of the others had been turned away.

As for America, in 1948 Washington had welcomed their trade delegation. Now they, too, had obviously changed their minds. The Dalai Lama felt great sorrow as he realized Tibet must expect to face the entire might of communist China alone. The Dalai Lama wanted, at all costs, to avoid the inevitable great loss of life and searched for a way this could be done.

He, and other officials, would often listen to the Tibetan language broadcasts of Radio Peking on an old radio receiver which ran off a 6-volt battery. The majority of the broadcasts were taken up with propaganda about the "Glorious Motherland," but the Dalai Lama was very impressed with much of what he heard. The constant talk of industrial progress and of the equality of all China's citizens seemed to the Dalai Lama like the perfect combination of material and spiritual progress.

One evening, however, as he listened alone, a harsh, crackling voice announced that a "Seventeen-Point Agreement" for the Peaceful Liberation of Tibet had that day been signed by representatives of the People's Republic of China and what they called the "Local Government" of Tibet.

The Dalai Lama was stunned. The two officials sent to Peking had no authority to sign any documents. The Dalai Lama had taken the state seals to safeguard against such a thing taking place. When internal information reached the Dalai Lama, he learned how the officials were forced to sign the "Agreement" under duress and use counterfeit seals of the Tibetan state.

The existence of the Seventeen-Point Agreement brought pressure on the Dalai Lama to return to Lhasa as soon as possible, and he soon agreed it was the right decision. In contrast to his journey to Droma, the journey back was very open. The Dalai Lama did not hurry, but took time to hold religious meetings and enjoy the coming of summer. He arrived in Lhasa in the middle of August after a nine-month absence. It looked like the entire population had turned out to welcome him back.

As the Chinese continued to move more and more troops and officials into Lhasa, conditions continued to deteriorate. Soon all supplies were short of demand. Wide-spread suffering of the Tibetans became very evident, and the Dalai Lama had no power to remedy the situation.

To ease their suffering and still not compromise his responsibility to his people, the Dalai Lama tried to pacify the Chinese officials by attempting to carry out some points of the Seventeen-Point Agreement. He soon learned it was impossible to speak his spiritual truth in the presence of the new Chinese master. He found the difficult circumstances made it necessary to put on a false appearance when dealing with the Chinese.

In early 1954, the Dalai Lama was invited to meet with Chairman Mao in China. Although few Tibetans were happy with the idea, it seemed to the Dalai Lama that it would be an excellent opportunity to discuss Tibet's needs, as well as broaden his knowledge of the outside world. He made up his mind to go regardless of the consequences.

One mid-summer morning the Dalai Lama — along with a retinue of about five hundred, which included his family, his two tutors, two tsenshap, the Kashag and a great many other officials — started the journey. They left Lhasa by crossing the Kyichu River.

There was still no bridge, so they crossed in animal-skin coracles. As the Dalai Lama climbed aboard his own special vessel, which consisted of two of these coracles strapped together, he turned and waved to the throng that had gathered to say goodbye. Many were convinced he would not return. Although the Dalai Lama felt sadness at their plight, the prospect of the adventure ahead was very thrilling to a young man of nineteen.

The distance from Lhasa to Peking was almost two thousand miles. In 1954 there were still no roads connecting the two countries. The Chinese, using forced Tibetan labor, had begun work on one called the Qinghai Highway. The part that was completed enabled the Dalai Lama to travel the first short distance in the thirteenth Dalai Lama's Dodge car.

The first stop was a garden monastery, about 35 miles from Lhasa, where they remained for a few days before embarking on horseback along the hazardous route the Chinese escort preferred rather than the traditional high altitude route.

There were no connecting roads to follow. Many bridges were down. There was constant flooding from mountain streams carrying melted snow. There were also frequent landslides. The heavy summer rains turned some areas to mud deep enough to come halfway to a person's knees. The older people had to struggle to keep up. The Tibetan guides tried to persuade the Chinese escorts to alter the course; that advice was not taken.

About two weeks out, they reached a small town called Demo and camped by a stream for the night. The weather was perfect, and the Dalai Lama was enchanted at the sight of the river banks adrift with yellow buttercups and mauve pink primulas. It was a sharp contrast to their usual overnight stops at military outposts manned by the PLA and bedecked with red flags.

Ten days later they were in the Payul region, where the road was again driveable. They were glad to give up the four-legged mode of travel as all of the pilgrims had painful backsides.

At this distance from Lhasa, they could see the Chinese were in effective control of the country. Many barracks had been built for their soldiers and houses for their officers. At Chambo, because the Chinese administered the place directly, the large reception had a very curious flavor. Military bands played hymns of praise to Chairman Mao and to the Revolution, and Tibetans stood waving red flags.

The hill at Dhan tse Idho marks the historic border between Tibet and China. As they descended to the plains on the other side on the way to Chengdu, the first town in China proper, the Dalai Lama remarked how different the countryside was. He wondered if the Chinese people would prove to be as different from the Tibetans as this countryside was from Tibet.

The travelers were to experience so many contrasts in modes of travel — some uncomfortable and crude — that it was difficult to remember just how many changes had been made. The last leg of the journey, they traveled by train. The carriages for the Dalai Lama were equipped with every facility imaginable, from beds and bathrooms to an elaborate dining car.

The Dalai Lama received a welcome in accordance with his importance. He stepped off the train at the station to be welcomed by a large crowd of young people. It did not take him long to realize their smiles and cheers were false. This added more anxiety to his growing sense of apprehension.

Still he was pleased with the accommodation assigned to him, a bungalow with a beautiful garden, which had previously belonged to the Japanese diplomatic mission.

The Dalai Lama's first two meetings with Mao Tse Tung were at a very formal banquet and a public meeting with format similar to the banquet.

The Dalai Lama described Chairman Mao as a "most impressive man. Physically he was extraordinary, his complexion was very dark, but his skin seemed shiny. It was as if he used some kind of ointment. His hands, which were beautiful with perfect fingers and an exquisitely formed thumb, had the same curious sheen as well."

The Dalai Lama also observed that Mao must have had some health problems. He had difficulty with breathing, and panted a great deal. His speech was very slow and precise. His mannerisms were similarly slow. He had a very emphatic air of authority and sincerity. His mere presence commanded respect.

The Dalai Lama spent about 10 weeks in China, and had at least a dozen meetings with Chairman Mao, most of which were at large gatherings. A few were private with only Phuntsog Wangyal in attendance acting as interpreter. Whatever the occasion, whether it was a banquet or a conference, Mao always made the Dalai Lama sit next to him.

The more the Dalai Lama looked at Marxism, the more he liked it. Here was a system based in equality and justice for everyone. Its only drawback seemed to be the insistence on a purely materialistic view of human existence. This he could not agree with. Even with his concerns he expressed his desire to become a party member. He felt then, and continued to feel, that it would be possible to work out a synthesis of Buddhist and pure Marxist doctrines that would prove to be a way of conducting politics.

When the First Assembly of the Communist Party took place, the Dalai Lama was made a vice president of the Steering

Committee of the People's Republic of China. This was a nominal appointment that carried some prestige, if not actually any political power. (The Steering Committee discussed policy before it was put up to the politburo, where the real power lay.)

The Dalai Lama's first impression of Mao as being sincere and genuine gradually gave way to doubt. During one private meeting, Mao told the Dalai Lama how glad he was the Dalai Lama had come to Peking. Mao said the purpose of China's presence in Tibet was to help. He said Tibet had fallen behind and China wanted to help. The Dalai Lama was skeptical, but Mao seemed to be speaking out of conviction. During one private conference with Mao he was surprised when Mao made favorable comments about the Lord Buddha, praising him for being anti-caste, anti-corruption and anti-exploitation. Suddenly Mao seemed to be pro-religion.

In their last private meeting before the Dalai Lama returned to Tibet, Mao wanted to give the Dalai Lama some advice about government. He proceeded to explain to the young Dalai Lama how to organize meetings, how to draw out people's opinions and then how to reach decisions. It was all excellent information. The Dalai Lama sat busily taking notes as always.

Mao drew closer to the Dalai Lama and said, "Your attitude is good, you know. Religion is poison. Firstly, it reduces the population (monks must stay celibate); and secondly, it neglects material progress."

At this the Dalai Lama was suddenly very afraid. So, he thought, you are the destroyer of the Dharma after all. He felt a violent burning sensation over his face. Fortunately Mao ended the interview after only a few more minutes.

Until that moment, the Dalai Lama had felt there could be a peaceful solution to the occupation of Tibet by the Communists. Now he knew that Mao had completely misjudged him. Mao had ignored the Buddha's instruction that anyone who practices the Dharma should test for themselves its validity. For this reason the Dalai Lama had always been open to the discoveries and truths of modern science.

Perhaps this openness had fooled Mao into thinking that the Dalai Lama's religious practices were nothing more than a prop or convention. It seemed to the Dalai Lama that political life in China was full of contradictions.

The Dalai Lama had remained in Peking until October, about 10 weeks. Although he and his entourage were taken on lengthy tours to see the industrial and material progress of China, he was never permitted to have contact with ordinary Chinese people. Every time he attempted to break away from the programer just to get out and see places for himself, he was prevented from doing so — always on the pretext of security. Fortunately one member of the entourage managed to get out and about. The Dalai Lama was thus able to get an intimate picture of what life was like in the brave, new People's Republic. It was a very somber picture.

When the Dalai Lama and his entourage left Peking for the return journey to Tibet, progress was faster. The Qinghai Highway had been completed. He took the opportunity to stop in different places for two or three days at a time so he could meet with as many of his countrymen as possible. Although still optimistic that a peaceful solution could be reached, the Dalai

Lama knew that few of his entourage shared his attitude. The return of the Dalai Lama to Lhasa April 1, 1957, was a very emotional occasion.

The situation was fast deteriorating. By mid-summer there was open warfare throughout Kham and Amdo. The Freedom Fighters were increasing their numbers on a daily basis and becoming ever more audacious in their raids on the Chinese.

The methods the Chinese used to intimidate the Tibetan population were so abhorrent that the Dalai Lama did not want to believe what he knew was true. Only the report published in 1959 by the International Commission of Tourists factually described the extent of the cruelty and slaughter. Some methods used were crucifixion, vivisection, disemboweling, not to mention beheading and burning alive. The list of methods used was endless.

The Dalai Lama had become a prisoner within his own palace, and those near him and responsible for his safety started to make plans for his escape. Secrecy was imperative. Only his closest advisors were taken into the confidence of those responsible for the safe departure of the Dalai Lama and his immediate family, teachers, and attendants.

The final time and escape route was not divulged to the Dalai Lama until the night of departure. Even then, only a few disguised attendants accompanied the Dalai Lama as they crept from the palace impersonating inspectors and moved through the throngs that had been standing vigil around the Potala to protect the Dalai Lama from his enemies.

The Dalai Lama removed his glasses to further improve his disguise, but since he was nearly blind without glasses, this impeded his progress and made traveling through the crowd torturous.

The Dalai Lama's small group of impersonators was to rendezvous with the rest of the company some distance from the city.

Messengers had been sent ahead requesting permission to exile to India. The journey was long, dangerous and depressing.

The flight of the Dalai Lama to India left a political vacuum greatly to the advantage of the Chinese who for the first time were able to seize a position of control in Lhasa and attack the heart of Tibet, even firing on the Potala.

The Chinese military took full advantage of the chaotic period that followed to increase their numerical strength in Tibet and to bolster their position in Lhasa.

For their part the Chinese seemed to have won over enough of the people to provide a limited supply of puppet officials.

The Tibetan Pontiff has repeatedly expressed a desire to return but not on present Chinese terms, which would restore his religious authority but not temporal powers.

The Dalai Lama had learned a lot about Chinese blandishment while a guest of Mao Tse Tung in Peking when he was young and impressionable. He is now less innocent in evaluating the motives of his adversaries.

In many respects the plight of Tibet was ignored by the world at large. The goal of independence was probably a mirage from the onset. However, the Dalai Lama's increased prestige as a recipient of the Noble Peace Prize has renewed world interest in the Tibetan situation and should intensify their struggle for self determination.

The Dalai Lama had some suggestions as to possible solutions and important contributions his country could make toward the peaceful cohabiting of countries bordering Tibet.

In his Five-Point Peace Plan, delivered on Capital Hill September 21, 1987, the proposals the Dalai Lama outlined were as follows:

1.   The transformation of the whole of Tibet into a zone of peace.
2.   Abandonment of China's population policy which threatens the very existence of the Tibetans as a people.
3.   Respect for the Tibetan people's fundamental human rights and democratic freedoms.
4.   Restoration and protection of Tibet's natural environment and abandonment of China's use of Tibet for the production of nuclear weapons and dumping of nuclear waste.
5.   Commencement of earnest negotiations on the future relations between Tibetan and Chinese people.

His final proposal was that the whole of Tibet be transformed into a zone of Ahisma (A Hindu term meaning a state of peace and non-violence). It would be, with Nepal's similar move to proclaim itself a peace zone, something that had already drawn China's support.

If implemented, it would allow Tibet to resume its historical role of acting as a neutral buffer state separating the continent's great powers.

The following are key points of the proposed zone of Ahisma:

The entire Tibetan plateau would be demilitarized.

The manufacture, testing and stockpiling of nuclear weapons and other armaments on the Tibetan plateau would be prohibited.

The Tibetan plateau would be transformed into the world's largest natural park or biosphere. Strict laws would be enforced to protect wild life and plant life. The exploitation of natural resources would be carefully regulated so as not to damage relevant ecosystems, and a policy of sustainable development would be adopted in populated areas.

Organizations dedicated to the furtherance of peace and to the protection of all forms of life would find a hospitable home in Tibet.

The establishment of international and regional organizations for the promotion and protection of human rights would be encouraged in Tibet.

A restoration of good relations between the world's two most populous countries would be greatly facilitated if they were separated, as they have been through out history, by a large and friendly intermediary region.

To improve relations between the Tibetan people and the Chinese, the first requirement is the creation of trust. Almost one and a quarter million Tibetans lost their lives from starvation, execution, torture and suicide. Tens of thousands lingered in prison camps. Only a withdrawal of Chinese troops could start a genuine process of reconciliation.

These proposals put forth by the Dalai Lama are sincere efforts of the rightful leader of a country that for generations has endeavored to live in harmony with its neighbors, whose only ambition is to be allowed to exist and worship in peace.

I have closely followed the terrible rape of Tibet since my visits there, I have been amazed and angered at the indifference that has been displayed by the great governments of the free world. How could we let this happen to a peaceful non-violent country like Tibet?

My main concern is that the recent Tiananmen Square massacre in Bejing, China, has over-shadowed the Tibetan tragedy. Actually here is a country the size of Western Europe which is getting neither the attention nor support that it deserves. I, for one, would like to raise my voice in outrage at the neglect and indifference manifested, by the US government in particular, in this matter.

The Dalai Lama has lived in exile in India since 1959, spending the time not required to fulfill his religious responsibilities working to bring to the attention of the world the appalling annihilation of the Tibetan people. Tibet is defenseless against the Chinese.

Tibet has, for forty years, been under foreign occupation. Today more than a quarter of a million Chinese troops are stationed in Tibet. Some sources estimate the occupation army to be twice this strength. During this time Tibetans have been deprived of their most basic human rights, including the right to life, movement, speech, worship, to mention only a few. More than one-sixth of Tibet's population of six million died as a direct result of the Chinese invasion and occupation.

The recent collapse of the Soviet Union brings new hope to the world that communist systems everywhere, including China, will fail, bringing freedom to all people of the world.

Only recently has there been any effort by the outraged people of the world to coordinate their work to free Tibet. Under the title of "The International Campaign for Tibet," a nonprofit organization based in Washington, D.C., is working to educate governments and people around the world on current conditions in Tibet.

The articles and material that follows in the Appendix of my series should be interesting and helpful to any and all civilized people. We must all pass the word that this great wrong must be reversed.

"The International Campaign of Tibet," working through all legal channels, needs our help.

I have used material from the Dalai Lama's recent book, "Freedom in Exile," in this book to update my narrative about Tibet and its struggle for freedom. The book is a marvelous account of his life in Tibet and later in exile in India.

The Silent Killing of Tibet

The Tibetans have an unusual procedure for disposing of their dead: sky burial. The corpses are carried up to craggy hilltops, hacked into little pieces, and fed to lammergeiers, a huge, brown species of vulture. There are practical reasons for this ancient custom: The ground is frozen much of the time and is too rocky for grave digging, and there's no wood for funeral pyres on the 12,000-foot Tibetan Plateau — trees are an event, and the only fuel is yak chips. But, most important, sky burial is rooted in the Buddhist belief that the body is nothing more than a temporary housing and, once vacated, has no further importance, so rather than letting it go to waste it is cycled back into the food chain and presented as a gift to our fellow sentient beings, the lammergeiers.

When the Forbidden Country was finally opened to tourism, in 1983, camera-clicking foreigners naturally flocked to the sky-burial sites. For several seasons they were tolerated, but one day a party of particularly pushy voyeurs was stoned by some grieving relatives, and ever since then the sites have been off-limits. The burials still go on, however, half a dozen a day in Greater Lhasa, my Tibetan guide was telling me as we looked up at the most popular site, behind the gilded pagodas of the Sera Monastery. These days, he confided, the bodies are often those of young monks or nuns arrested for protesting against the Chinese. The men who do the dismembering are experienced at recognizing things out of the ordinary, and they report cracked ribs, kidney damage, and other evidence of torture.

This jibes with the findings of various human-rights groups: One of the largest genocides any country has ever perpetrated on another continues. Since the Chinese invaded the country in 1951, an estimated 1.2 million Tibetans — one-fifth of the population — have died of unnatural causes. Though the Chinese have been trying to appear more humane and lifted martial law a year after the Tiananmen massacre of June 1989, this seems to be no more than a public-relations ploy. All kinds of atrocities are still going on. Paramedic teams are sterilizing entire villages. Pregnant women are being dragged screaming into hospitals and forcibly aborted. Chinese obstetricians are administering lethal injections into the soft spots of newborn babies' heads. Nuns, who have come to the forefront of the freedom movement in recent months, are being stripped naked, mauled by dogs, and violated with electric cattle prods. The new thing in the prisons is forcing inmates to give blood "donations" three times a day, releasing them, if at all, only when they are almost completely exsanguinated and at the point of death.

Just as appalling is the fact that the systematic annihilation of the Tibetan people and their culture is taking place, for reasons of superpower realpolitik, without a word of protest from the leaders of the free world, those champions of liberty who are supposed to rush to the aid of small helpless states when they are gobbled up by their big nasty neighbors. Because of their Buddhist pacifism. Tibetans are virtually defenseless against the Chinese occupation, which Aleksandr Solzhenitsyn has described as the most brutal Communist regime on the planet. "In general, we Tibetans are very religious-minded," the Dalai Lama, the country's exiled spiritual and temporal leader, reflected not long ago. "But believing the country would be saved without human effort, through prayers alone, resulted from limited knowledge. From this point of view, religious sentiment actually became an obstacle."

CIRCUMAMBULATING

Every Tibetan wants, more than anything, to go to Lhasa, the capital of this vast, spectacular land hidden behind the Himalayas, a third the size of China; to see the Potala, the sumptuous 1,200-room palace where the fifth through the present Dalai Lamas lived; and to circumambulate the Jokhang, the great central temple in the city's heart, built by Songsten Gampo, the seventh-century king who adopted Buddhism. In the early eighties the Chinese lifted their ban on public worship in Tibet. But they had no idea that the religion was still so strong, that virtually 100 percent of the population was still *nangpa*, "within the faith," and continued to revere the Dalai Lama as the fourteenth incarnation of their ruling archangel even though he had been driven out of the country in 1959 and none of the younger generation had ever set eyes on him. It was he who held together what was left of the Tibetan identity here and abroad, and a pageant of pent-up-devotion, the likes of which had not been seen in the West since the days of Chaucer, soon reclaimed the land.

A decade later, the whole population seems to be on a pilgrimage. Wherever there's a shrine or a holy place to be circumambulated, a ring of Tibetans are usually shuffling around it, murmuring mantras, twirling prayer wheels, generating good karma for their next incarnation. The monasteries are full of long, swaying, softly humming, conga lines of true believers, their awestruck faces illuminated by blazing rows of yak-butter lamps as

they make their way from room to room full of gaudy Buddhist art. Many are tall, red-cheeked, ready-smiling members of the Khampa tribe, from eastern Tibet. The women are decked out in massive turquoise and red coral jewelry and red-tasseled braids. The men wear long black robes, with silver daggers and charm boxes on their belts, and both sexes sport pastel-colored high sneakers from the People's Republic of China, to which they are supposed to belong. They have been on the road for days, weeks, months. Some have prostrated the whole way, measuring the tarmac like inchworms; moving their hands, pressed together in prayer on top of their head, down to their throat, to their heart, then dropping to their knees and keeling forward so that every part of their body embraces the sacred earth, then getting up, spitting out the dust, striding forward a body length, and repeating the process.

The inner circuit of the Jokhang is known as the Barkhor and takes about twenty minutes to perform, if you keep moving. But there are many distractions, for the Barkhor is also the liveliest bazaar, the Times Square of Tibet, and the center of national life, swarming with all kinds of people. Pickpockets, street kids, and pretty girls done up in turquoise and coral mingle in the slowly turning throng of devotees with pale, edgy, baby-faced Chinese soldiers and *gyan-yi* — plainclothes operatives of the dread Chinese Public Security Bureau posing as beggars or itinerant monks (you can tell who they are because they wear shades and periodically raise side bags containing walkie-talkies to their ears).

If anything is going to happen, if there is to be another outburst of reactionary counter-revolutionary secessionism, it will probably be here, in the Barkhor. Like the flare-up of September 1987, in which twenty-one young circumambulating monks suddenly raised the outlawed Tibetan flag (two snow lions against snow peaks) and began chanting for independence. A few days later, an angry crowd stormed the police station where the monks were being held and set it on fire. Or the riot in March of the following year, in which three Chinese policemen were stoned to death, and four Tibetans, one of them a fifteen-year-old monk, were gunned down — after which Beijing's policy of "merciless repression" was imposed. Or the demonstrations in May 1989, which resulted in the deaths of 16 or 800 Tibetans (depending on which side's tally you subscribe to).

My new friend Jules, with whom I was circumambulating the Barkhor one afternoon not long ago, motioned with his eyebrows up to a rooftop where two Chinese soldiers were standing in front of a mounted high-caliber machine gun and surveying the crowd. Jules was an antiques smuggler who specialized in Ming porcelain. We had flown to Lhasa together from Kathmandu, Nepal. I had come in squeaky-clean — no Dalai Lama pictures, nothing to suggest, with my binoculars and field guides to the birds, butterflies, and wildflowers of the Himalayas, that I was anything other than who I said I was: a naturalist. But Jules was playing a more dangerous game. He had gotten a sixty-day visa for China, booked a flight to Ch'eng-tu, the capital of neighboring Szechwan, and simply gotten off at Lhasa. When the P.S.B. officer at the airport asked for his Tibetan travel permit, he produced the visa and said ingenuously that he thought this was part of China. "At first the guy said I'd have to stay at the airport and take the next flight out," Jules was telling me. "But after several glasses of cognac and a ten-dollar bill slipped discreetly into his jacket pocket, he started to tell me the story of his life. There was an electric cattle prod on the table between us, the kind the P.S.B. routinely uses for interrogation, I picked it up and asked, What's this thing?"

"A shock," he said.

"Did you ever try it yourself? See what it feels like? I jabbed it at him and he shrank back in terror. Then next morning he put me in a car to Lhasa.

Being the only *inji,* as Westerners are known in Tibetan (from "English-man"), in sight, we were objects of wide-eyed curiosity, particularly from some Golok nomads who had flown in from a vast, practically uninhibited prairie the size of Colorado known as the Changthang, "the northern grassy solitudes." Three women danced around us holding up turquoise-and-coral necklaces, earrings, and amulets, and asking cheerily, "Hello how much? Come on, Your last how much?" One of them pinched me encouragingly on the butt, "You too much," I told her.

You wouldn't have guessed from the high spirits of the Tibetans what they have been through, or that they are living in a very ugly police state. Everything seems calm in the Barkhor, even festive. A group of Hor nomad girls were gaily spinning a row of cylindrical bronze prayer wheels along the wall of the shrine with the absorption of teenagers in a video parlor. Tibetan Buddhism has tremendous entertainment value. As a lama in Kathmandu put, it is the Disneyland of religions.

The faces of these people are extraordinary — so different from the pallid masks that the Chinese soldiers wear. When Tibetans smile, their eyes widen, the skin draws back, and their whole face expands and lights up like a bulb. Contentment and untroubled clarity radiate from their features, maybe because of their practice of the system for overcoming the suffering of existence that a Hindu prince named Siddhartha worked out 2,500 years ago after years of acetic ordeals, finally becoming a Buddha, or enlightened being. In the 1,200 years since the system reached Tibet, it has been refined in monasteries that produced their own Einsteins and Freuds, who did their research on inner science, tearing consciousness apart and scrutinizing it under clinical conditions. One Western practitioner describes the set of specific meditations and visualizations that compose Tibetan Buddhism as "not so much a religion as a completely down-to-earth and practical science of mind. The Tibetans deal with the mind in a very profound way. They are masters of one-pointedness and interiorization, and until you get the mind sorted out you can't get anywhere in your spiritual practice."

But one of the main teachings of the Buddha is that out-ward appearances are illusory, and so it is possible that the people in the Barkhor, outwardly all smiles and laughter, are seething inside, that what the circumambulators are chanting under their breath is not the famous core mantra, *Om Mane Padme Hum* ("The Jewel in the Lotus"), but actually "Chinese, Go Home," and that this whole, overpowering pageant of devotion, which seems to be the only thing happening in Tibet, is actually a subtle kind of nonviolent mass protest, and underneath the apparent calm is a volcano.

We pass a distinguished-looking old man wearing a lapel button that reads, to our amazement, I LOVE TIBET. FREE TIBET. I ask Rinchen, the hip young exile from the tour company who came in with me to see everything goes smoothly, to drop back and discretely get the man's views. A few minutes later, Rinchen catches up with us. "I asked the old man how the situation was, and he said it's like being a dog that is taken around everywhere on a leash. You can't bring out your sorrow. Smoke can't come out your nostrils no matter how big the fire is in your heart."

THE EMPIRE STRIKES BACK

In front of the Jokhang Temple is a stone monument commemorating a treaty concluded between Tibet and China in 821-22 A.D., in which both parties agreed to stay for the next 10,000 years in their respective countries: "Tibetans shall be happy in the land of Tibet, and Chinese shall be happy in the land of China."

But it didn't work out that way. There are two widely divergent versions of what happened in the subsequent millennium, of the complex saga of Sino-Tibetan relations. Some blame the fifth Dalai Lama — the Great Fifth, who built the Potala — for renewing the dormant patron-priest relationship with Beijing established in the days of Kublai Khan, and thus placing Tibet under Chinese suzerainty.

Robert Thurman, a professor of Indo-Tibetan studies at Columbia University, has a different take. Thurman was the first American to be ordained as a Tibetan monk. He later derobed ("I realized the monk trip was really self-indulgent on my part and I should try to hack it in the world") and married a Swedish high-fashion model. Their second child, Uma, is the sultry star of Henry & June.

"Central Asia was one of

the world's great warlord breeding grounds." Thurman explained. "It spawned many of the world's conquering empires — the Tibetan empire of the first millennium: the Mongols, whose empire was the biggest in world history; the Ottomans, who were descended from the Uighurs of East Turkestan, immediately to the north of Tibet. So the lamas of Tibet were quite aware of the military nature of nations.

"In the seventeenth century," Thurman went on, "the Oirat Mongols, who were 20 million strong, spread to the Black Sea, and they tried to win the Great Fifth to their vision of a Pan-Tibetan-Mongolian bloc that would stand up to the Manchus, who were taking over China. But the Fifth realized that a Mongol alliance would keep Tibet in the medieval pattern of a highly militaristic feudal nobility and a monastic elite, and he didn't want that, so he asked the farthest-away guy, who almost never came to Tibet, for a loose hegemony: let the Manchus keep the peace in central Asia. In so doing he bought Tibet three centuries to practice the dharma undisturbed, and Tibet developed from a normally ethnocentric, warlike, imperialistic national culture to a universally Buddhicized, spiritual, peaceful culture. Tibet evolved a unique personality constellation which I call 'inner modernity' — as advanced as the West is in 'outer modernity,' as extremely inward as we are outward.

"The Fifth in fact created an extraordinary social experiment: a state with zero pollution, zero population growth due to the voluntary celibacy of 20 percent of the males, no military budget, and a completely harmonious relationship with its wildlife, its environment, and its neighbors. Isn't that what we're all looking for?"

But wasn't Tibet pollution-free because it was pre-industrial? I asked.

"On the contrary," Thurman countered, "it was an industrial society. The monasteries were factories, streamlined assembly lines for the most important product there can be — enlightened beings. But the only problem." Thurman conceded, "was that the Great Flfth also set things in motion for a society that couldn't defend itself. Whether he foresaw the destruction of the Buddhist state, whether he intended for Tibet to self-destruct — who knows? Who can know what goes on in the mind of an enlightened being?

"But the most important point in this discussion," he stressed, "is that in all the centuries that the Chinese claimed Tibet as part of their empire *they were never there!* China's claim was never more than a court fantasy. There is no documentary evidence to support it, while the documentary evidence that Tibet governed itself as an independent entity is extensive. It was like a delegation coming to Beijing from thousands of miles away and saying, We bring you England."

The first serious attempt to take possession of Tibet didn't happen until 1910, when an army sent by the Manchus took Lhasa, committing atrocities that now seem like a dress rehearsal for the current occupation. But a year later the Manchus were overthrown by the Nationalists, and Tibet was left more or less to itself until 1948, when the civil war in China ended with the Nationalists departing the mainland.

There were three things Mao Tsedung wanted badly: Taiwan, Korea, and Tibet. All he got was Tibet. In 1950, he sent an army to "liberate the oppressed and exploited Tibetans and reunite them with the great motherland," and also to protect them from the "forces of imperialism," which was a bit of a crock as there were only ten *inji* in the whole country and what was he doing there if not committing a blatant act of imperialism himself?

The general population responded to the threat with feverish prayer and circumambulation. The Dalai Lama, who was only fourteen, fled to the Indian border, taking with him more than a thousand pack animals laden with treasure. But a few months later he was persuaded by his spiritual advisers, including the state oracle (who goes into a trance whenever an important decision has to be made), to return to Lhasa and try to work something out with Mao. The two leaders didn't meet until 1954. The Dalai Lama had seen the possibilities for a synthesis between Buddhism and Marxism, but ended up deciding that Mao was "'an enemy of the dharma."

When he returned to Lhasa, the Dalai Lama found that the liberation had taken an ugly turn. The Chinese army and Tibetan riffraff they had recruited were relieving people of their arms, livestock, and other possessions. Everything was being collectivized. Prominent families were being bound and dragged to the village squares for *thamzing,* or "struggle sessions," and were being forced to confess to their crimes against the people," and those whose performance was unsatisfactory were being executed on the spot. The Khampa went on the warpath, and the Dalai Lama, who wanted to emulate Gandhi's nonviolence, despaired. He had lost control of the country.

In 1959 there was a major insurrection in Lhasa. Tens of thousands of Tibetans surrounded the Norbulingka Palace to protect the Dalai Lama from the Chinese, whose program was now clear. Their commander had invited him to a soiree at the barracks. Perhaps they would fox-trot to Bing Crosby records, which was the rage with Lhasa's smart set. But he was to come alone, without his guards. Under the cover of night and in disguise, the Dalai Lama and his family fled south again, the People's Liberation Army hot on their heels, and he barely made it, across the Indian border. A hundred thousand Tibetans,

including the cream of society and the Lamaist hierarchy, followed, and at least 87,000 of those who stayed behind were slaughtered.

Three months later, in India, the Dalai Lama gave his first press conference, in which he claimed that China's true aim was "the extermination of the religion and culture and even the absorption of the Tibetan race."

The atrocities, which began in 1957, reached a peak during the Cultural Revolution years, from 1966 to 1977. Entire villages were obliterated, their residents crucified or disemboweled, burned or boiled alive, or dragged from the backs of horses. Children were forced to shoot their parents, disciples their teachers, nuns to copulate publicly with monks and to desecrate sacred images. All but 40 of the country's 6,254 monasteries were gutted, and their treasure — $80 billion worth of ancient *thankas* and gold and silver — was shipped back in endless truck convoys to the motherland, where it made its way through Hong Kong to European auction houses and private collectors. Thousands of bundles of woodblock-printed scripture — 1,200 years of research on the inner workings of the mind — were burned. In the monasteries that weren't razed, huge portraits of Chairman Mao, looking like Big Brother, were put up. Tens of thousands of Tibetans were marched off to a growing string of labor camps in the North, South, and East that made the Gulag look like Playland. Inmates were reduced to fighting over the maggots in each other's excrement. Only hundreds survived. Their appalling conditions are chronicled in John Avedon's powerful book, *In Exile from the Land of Snows.*

There are incredible stories from this period: high *tulkus* (recognized incarnations of "perfection-stage adepts," who, in theory, can choose the time, place, and womb of their rebirth) under torture stopping to inhale and shooting their consciousness out of their body and into their next manifestation. Avedon focuses on the ordeal of Tenzin Choedrak, now the Dalai Lama's senior physician, who survived twenty years in prison and labor camps by murmuring millions of mantras and practicing advanced *tum-mo* heat-generating meditation, which helped him stay alive in his freezing cell and break down the barely digestible fare.

At the same time, there was an all-out onslaught on every other form of life in the country. Untold millions of sentient beings were liberated from their temporary consciousness housings. Cats, caged birds, and lovable golden Lhasa Apsos were exterminated for being parasites and undesirable relics of past society. Songbirds were shot out of trees, the excuse being that they destroyed crops, but actually because they are a Chinese delicacy. By all accounts, the wild animals in Tibet, having never been molested, had been incredibly tame and approachable. Now huge flocks of Brahminy ducks, bar-headed geese, and black-necked cranes (of which only a few hundred are left), herds of kiang (wild ass). drong (wild yak), antelope, gazelle, and blue sheep were machine-gunned and cooked up by the occupying forces. The vast virgin forests of eastern Tibet were clear-cut and an estimated $54 billion worth of pine, rhododendron, larch, and oak was added to the endless stream of trucks. The entire subcontinent is still shuddering from the ecological repercussions of this massive deforestation — including floods in Bangladesh and alteration of the monsoons.

One wonders how much of Mao's liberation was motivated by simple covetousness. The name the Chinese gave to their newly annexed territory — Xizang — is telling: it means "Our Western Treasure-House." It had fertile farmland in the East and South, uranium, lithium, tungsten, borax, and gold, more than ninety totally unexploited resources, strategic importance — whoever controlled the Tibetan Plateau looked down on the rest of Asia — and above all, for the billion-plus Han masses, space.

With the death of Chou

En-lai in 1976, the oppression in Tibet eased up a bit. Some Chinese began to realize that horrible mistakes had been made in the way Tibet had been treated. By the early eighties it became clear that Beijing was not going to break the back of Tibetan culture. The Old Guard had all died and the cultural lobotomy was aborted. The new policy was: You can have your religion, you can have your dogs (there was a tremendous resurgence of canines, though not the Lhasa Apsas — Nepalese strays, pariah dogs, which have become a real problem around the monasteries). We won't bother you too much, but we won't give you decent jobs or an education either. As long as you accept your degraded status everything will be fine, but if you demonstrate, if you start clamoring for Tibetan independence, you will be cracked down on severely.

But the genocide of the Tibetans by absorption continues. Han Chinese were given generous incentives to settle in Xizang and were rewarded for marrying Tibetan women. Currently, the Han-Tibetan ratio on the plateau is estimated to be 7.5 million to 6 million.

HAPPY
HAPPY
HAPPY

The Lhasa Holiday Inn is a multi-million-dollar extravaganza the Chinese have sunk into Tibetan tourism, and it dominates the sterile, creepily 1984-like Chinese new town that has taken over much of the Happy River Valley, where Lhasa used to be. Tourism is about the only money-making proposition that the Chinese have going in Xizang, which puts the tourist in an awkward position because he is in effect subsidizing the oppression. On the other hand, tourists joined the demonstrations of the late eighties and can be credited with arousing in the Tibetans bourgeois capitalist cravings for things like self-determination and individual rights.

So far, the tourists have not arrived in great enough number to undermine the culture, to turn the pageant of devotion into a replica of itself, as eventually happens (look at Carnival in Rio, for instance). They are still outnumbered hundreds to one in the conga lines at the monasteries. Besides Jules and me there were a group of elderly Americans, gutsy widows who have taken it into their heads to see Tibet before they

die, a German group (Tibet is the sort of place Germans go for — Hitler believed the masters of the universe, the old arcane sages, lived here), a young Brazilian named Marcos who was traveling around the world, and a couple of people like me and Jules, whose presentations didn't quite add up, among them a French diplomat who was right out of *Casablanca*, smoking coolly and traveling on a regular passport as a "manager."

The Lhasa Holiday Inn has to be one of the most remote and surreal bastions of modernity in the hemisphere, if not the sphere. But Tibet as a touristic experience — the monasteries choked with pilgrims, the dust-, glare-, and altitude-heightened Chaucerian time warp — was so intense and out of this world that I found myself feeling almost grateful for the amenities the hotel offered. It was a lifeline for the discombobulated *inji*, with its hot, running water, nightly videos — *Perry Mason* reruns, James Bond, *One Flew over the Cuckoo's Nest* — on the TV, Coke (which had beaten Pepsi to the plateau but was no more the Real Thing than the local version of Kent cigarettes). Something had also been lost in translation in the arrangements of Beethoven's Ninth and "Home on the Range" that emanated incessantly from overhead speakers: they sounded exactly the same. The Han Chinese who tried to run the place up to American standards all looked the same. They were nonindividuated, programmed porcelain dolls, like the girl who greeted me with a mechanical smile and the words "Coupon, please" at the dining-room door, and the younger set at the disco; a dozen girls dancing in formation like aerobics class, soldiers in uniform box-stepping together to hot numbers like Rick Dee's 1976 novelty hit, "Disco Duck," Marcos had the perfect word for the scene: "*massificado,*" mentally massified. Happy music gushing all day long on the banks of the Happy River, happy bees going about their little tasks, each contributing to the good of the hive, happy tourists, happy Tibetans, happy Han Chinese, everybody playing his part in the wary charade that life in Lhasa had become.

At night Rinchen and I would sneak out of the hotel and, tying on the white gauze masks that everyone wore because of the dust, we would flag down a bicycle rickshaw, be pedaled past undifferentiated concrete apartment blocks, barracks, and office buildings, all in the same sterile party architecture, to the Tibetan quarter on the other side of town, where the Barkhor was, where the action was. There, in dark little dives straight out of *Indiana Jones*, we would hear that things were not so great after all.

One time we were led down the dark, rickety, second-story walkway of an ancient, tilting building and seated on a hokey sofa in a low-ceilinged, dirt-floored living room. As the handsome daughter of the house poured us cup after cup of salty, rancid yak-butter tea (definitely an acquired taste), we were told that Tibetans were becoming outcasts, second-class citizens in their own land, like Native Americans or Australian aborigines. It was very hard for a Tibetan to proceed beyond high school because everything at the college level was taught in Mandarin. So there were the

beginnings of a hang-out problem. No drugs or prostitution yet, but mahjongg had sifted down to the masses (in the old Tibet, noblemen had gone on mahjongg binges that lasted for days), and the young blades were playing billiards, smoking, and sometimes stealing to get along. The Chinese were making cheap radish liquor and rice booze available, perhaps in a deliberate effort to addict young Tibetans, as we did our Indians. It was also Chinese policy to encourage inter-Tibetan violence. Pickpockets and robbers were given lenient prison terms — half weren't even sentenced. Truly disruptive elements were recruited as *gyan-yi* — "undressed police" — by the P.S.B.

We know the young monks and nuns are for the Dalai Lama and Tibetan independence, I told the man of the house, but what about the others?

"There's no difference between the monks and the laity," he answered. "All have the same feeling." But later in the evening, he said, "Sixty percent believe in freedom, 20 percent don't care, and 20 percent — those who play footsie with the Chinese — don't want it."

And how will Tibet gain its freedom, with the Dalai Lama ruling out violence?

Pause, Rinchen translates; "He believes it's not possible. Only if China falls apart again, as it did when the Manchus were overthrown in 1911."

KATHMANDU

One afternoon in Kathmandu I rode out to a transit camp for newly arrived Tibetan refugees on the back of a motorcycle with a young exile active in the freedom movement. I'll call him Sonam. Kathmandu has a thriving Tibetan community with a dozen-odd monasteries and several remarkable *tulkus.* A lot of Tibetans were coming over the border, Sonam told me, to attend a high-level teaching called the Kalachakra initiation, which the Dalai Lama was giving the following month at Sarnath, the city in India where the Buddha himself began to teach. "Most of them won't understand head or tail of the initiation, but they're hoping at least to get part of the blessing from the holy gathering, to catch a glimpse of the Dalai Lama."

The Chinese were issuing limited numbers of temporary travel permits — none to monks or nuns. False travel permits, which were actually hospital admission cards, were selling like hotcakes in Lhasa for two yuan a piece to illiterate devotees. The soldiers were tearing them up at the border. A lot were sneaking over without permits, hiding in the backs of trucks and hiring Nepali coyotes to guide them across, which was risky because some of the coyotes for a second fee turned the refugees back to the Chinese border guards. For those who already had a record of demonstrating, *refoulement* was death.

The son of nomads, Sonam had left Tibet in the '59 diaspora at the age of eight, he knew a great deal about the nomads' folk beliefs. He told me about some Lilliputian beings less than a foot tall, called *samishingmi,* who sat on mule dung for benches and used blades of grass for arrows. "When I was a kid, my parents told me not to roll boulders down the hill onto the prairie, because they would scratch the surface of the grass. There was a place called Crystal Hill where rock crystals sparkled in the sun, but we were forbidden to break them off because they were the toys of the spirit babies." He told me that turtles were believed to be reincarnated "miser men," who, having never offered hospitality to anyone in their previous lives, were condemned to carry their houses around wherever they went.

We turned up a path that ran between fields where women in vibrant saris were putting in their last crop of cauliflower and white radish. The Balagu refugee camp was a former factory: two stories of rooms facing an inner courtyard. In the mess hall, all of the hundred or so refugees were glued to a video of the Dalai Lama. Catching sight of me, some of the refugees put their tongues out, a traditional gesture of goodwill and respect which, Sonam explained, was originally intended to show that one was not a Bön practitioner, which was the shamanistic religion that preceded Buddhism, (those practitioners were said to have had blue tongues.)

I spent the afternoon debriefing small groups of refugees, one, composed of three young nuns from the Ani Tsangkhun Convent in Lhasa. With their shaven heads and round faces they were quite indistinguishable from the young monks, except their robes were brown, while the men's were maroon over saffron. Lobsang, a hefty twenty-year-old with an irrepressible smile and a sparkling gold eye-tooth, said that she and her friend had gone over the ice wall of the Himalayas, the most imposing natural barrier on the planet, nineteen days before.

In the next batch of three nuns, two couldn't stop giggling. The other looked grim, hurt, angry. It was clear that something terrible had happened. Her name was Kunsang, and she said she had spent six months in the Kutsa Prison for putting up posters. Her brother had been shot dead through the neck in the big March demonstration.

What was it like in the prison? "Everybody was tortured, except the snitches. Some went crazy. Only one-third of those who go to prison can come back to normal life. Two-thirds are permanently disabled. Our fellow nuns could bring us food once a month. I was stripped, kicked all over." Her lower lip began to quiver violently.

What now? I asked. "I have no personal plans, except to continue to fight for the cause of Tibetan freedom."

The video had ended and everyone was out in the courtyard enjoying the last hour of sun, laughing, playing cards. A dozen faces were pressed to the window. A rack of pleated, monsoon-slashed foothills rose in the background. Behind them stood the breathtaking white wall of the Ganesh Himal, and over the wall was Tibet — the forbidden country.

THE GREAT
FOURTEENTH

An old British hill station in Himachal Pradesh, India, 125 miles from the Tibet border, where the viceroy and his entourage summered in the heyday of the Raj, Dharamsala is now the seat of the Tibetan government in exile. A faint aura of the sixties hovers over the place. The flower children who hit the orphic trail to India in the late sixties and early seventies were among the first to discover Dharamsala and the Dalai Lama's message of global harmony through personal transformation. Hundreds of thousands never returned from the subcontinent (150,000 French alone, it is said), and, middle-aged now, they are part of the landscape like the Bakhtis, or Shiva seekers, and all the other indigenous varieties of wandering mendicant long-hair. The Tibetan medicine clinic of Yeshi Donden, the Dalai Lama's former personal physician, was packed with emaciated, toothless old dharma bums.

That there was an exile government that handles the problems of the refugees and is ready to return at a moment's notice should China collapse and the "liberators" leave was truly impressive, even though the inevitable court intrigues and power struggles had carried over from the ancient regime, the chain of address to His Holiness was jealously guarded, and, as Khandro Chazotsang, a woman in the Home Office in charge of the rehabilitation of new arrivals, told me, a "*babuji* element, the British-influenced clerk mentality that makes the Indian bureaucracy so impos-sible to deal with, had crept in.

The seed money for the exile government came from the treasure brought out by the thousand-plus pack animals in 1950, stashed in a stable in Sikkim, and cashed for — accounts vary — $1 million or $8 million. All Tibetan exiles everywhere (there is a sizable contingent in Switzerland, for instance) send contributions. The orphans at the Tibetan Children's Village above Macleod Ganj, run by one of the Dalai Lama's sisters, have individual sponsors. The Indian government gives relief, and there are some private Western donors. (Although it hasn't had a vogue the way the rain forest has, the Tibetan cause has ardent supporters ranging from Abe Rosenthal to Richard Gere.) The dollar goes a long way here.

But there is no help from the United States government. In the beginning, America perceived that the Tibetan freedom movement could be useful in the war against Communism and backed it, as it did the contras and the mujahideen. Tibetan freedom fighters, kept in the dark about where they were going, were flown to Camp Hale, Colorado, where they were trained by the C.I.A. under utmost secrecy in techniques of guerrilla warfare, armed with the latest sophisticated equipment, and flown back to the plateau. But then, in 1971, Henry Kissinger advised Nixon to buddy up to Mao so they could work together against the Russians, and aid to the freedom movement was abruptly terminated. A pawn in a larger power game, Tibet was sacrificed. Avedon relates how the guerrillas were hunted down and,

finally, sandwiched between Chinese and Napali troops, slaughtered, and how their bravest leaders, ordered by the Dalai Lama to desist from violence, slit their own throats rather than disobey him.

George Bush was Nixon's envoy to the People's Republic, and he remains its loyal fan. In 1977 he was taken to Lhasa and snowed by the Tibetan Revolutionary Museum, below the Potala, where amputated hands of criminals, flayed skin, implements of torture, human-thighbone trumpets monks had blown, and evidence of other alleged atrocities of the "liberated Lamaist feudal state" were on display. The State Department refused the Dalai Lama visas in 1960 and 1977 for fear of upsetting the Chinese. Finally, in 1979, he was let in, but to date no American president has dared to shake his hand. The Soviet peril has subsided, but China still contains a quarter of the world's market.

I had asked Tenzin Geyche Tethong, the Dalai Lama's private secretary, for permission to observe some of the other audiences His Holiness was having. It had been granted, and that afternoon I walked up to the Tegsum Choeling Temple, the main temple in Dharamsala, which is out on a spur of the ridge that overlooks the vast Kangra Valley, thousands of feet below. There was something almost sci-fi about the scene, like walking into this futuristic factory for enlightened beings. In the yard, pairs of young shaven-headed monks, in ritual combat stance, were thrusting their arms at each other. I thought they were practicing martial arts, but in fact it was dialectics. From inside the temple came the flatulent blats of long brass horns called *dung-chen* and the steady drone of oboe-like *gyaling*. I stepped through a gate guarded by Indian soldiers into the adjacent executive compound. A plain-clothes Tibetan frisked me and searched through my side bag. Nothing had happened yet, but there was always the danger of a crazy, like the one who shot Gandhi, getting through.

The audiences took place in a villa up the hill. The first was with a group of pilgrims — humble steppe people in tribal shawls who had come all the way from Ladakh for His Holiness's blessing. His Holiness came out on a veranda dripping with bougainvillea. He wore olive-tinted glasses and maroon monk's robes. The pilgrims approached him in a line, one by one, bent over, not daring to look at him. As a retainer held a black parasol over him, he also bent over and presented each of them with a blessing cord and a packet of blessed pills. All this happened in silence, broken occasionally by His Holiness asking in a rich, deep, resonant voice, questions like "Which route did you take?" grunting ruminatively, or breaking out in a basso burst of laughter. (The Dalai Lama has "a wonderful laugh," *The Washington Post* reported on his first American visit. "It surprises itself in the act of delight and rings out around the room, as if all his past thirteen incarnations were joining in." Then all the pilgrims backed away from him, taking a last longing look, some mumbling mantras a mile a minute, a few with tears of joy streaming down their cheeks. All this took no more than five minutes, although it seemed to be happening in slow motion.

As I watched this tableau of adoration, I reflected how the Dalai Lama could have spent the rest of his life living comfortably in the South of France, receiving the occasional visitor for tea. But instead he has been working tirelessly for his people, and indeed for all mankind. In 1989, he was awarded the Nobel Peace Prize, the only Asian to have won it on his own. The Chinese called the award "preposterous." Congratulations from the White House were not forthcoming.

The more I thought about his message, the more I was taken by it. His policy of Universal Responsibility, derived from the Buddhist kinship with all "sentient beings," contains the seeds for the salvation of the planet. He advocates a politics of compassion, not of chess — the old Machiavellian Kissinger approach which has brought us to the brink of self-immolation. The problem is, is anybody in power about to listen to him?

Maybe, I began to think, it was no mistake that the Dalai Lama was driven from his isolated land. Maybe he came out to help bring about the much discussed "new world order" — or what's left of it since the Baltic crackdown and the holy war in the Gulf — whatever meaning the term retains since it adoption by George Bush.

My first question, when the two of us were alone together, was about the new geopolitical shape the world is struggling to assume, how at the same time that it's growing together it's breaking up into small, independent states, re-Balkanizing. Lithuania, Latvia, Estonia, Georgia, Moldavia, want out of the Soviet Union. The Kashmiris and the Sikhs in the Punjab have no desire to be a part of India. Outer Mongolia (where the Dalai Lama is giving the Kalachakra initiation this summer) is already an autonomous satellite; opposition parties are allowed, there are free elections and a tremendous resurgence of Buddhism, which was crushed by the Bolsheviks. It's a model of hope for Tibet. The longing for self-determination is spreading into China. The Uighur Muslims in bordering East Turkestan are as eager for the Chinese to leave as the Tibetans are. The economic zones around Shanghai, having tasted free enterprise, would love to check out of the People's Republic as well. My question was: Suppose all these people actually get their freedom; is that really the instant formula for world peace? Won't it create new opportunities for territorial aggression and ethnic and sectarian strife? Won't everybody soon be back at each other's throats?

"Because of economic situation, world must come together on free basis, without losing individual identity," he replied in Pidgin English, devoid of unnecessary subjects, verbs and articles and amazingly effective and to the point. "Economy and ecology now extend beyond national borders. Soviet and Chinese collectiveships were imposed without freedom, so they won't work now. They're collapsing, aren't they? My idea is that war something old-fashioned. Everyone want peace. But peace not just absence of war. For forty years there has been no war in Europe, but this is not genuine peace. It has been out of fear of nuclear war. The new peace genuine because form

mutual respect.

"All continents must demilitarize, each individual nation, one by one. Europe will be first. But some mischievous elements will happen, so to protect there must be some kind of collective member-state force. Each state contribute same number of police, on rotation system, and everybody must stop making business from weapons. That is the real cause of instability in the Middle East and everywhere."

His recognition of the need for some kind of peacekeeping force was an important point, I thought. On many occasions the Dalai Lama had said things like, Your enemy is your best friend and should be a special focus of compassion, because it is he who makes you grow, and had claimed to be sincerely grateful to Mao for teaching him the realities of suffering and impermanence. This and the central doctrine of Buddhism that nothing is inherently real didn't seem very useful attitudes when someone is pointing a gun at you. But in fact surgical or preventive violence is not only allowed by the bodhisattva ethic, it is required. You must take out a mass murderer if you can, or you yourself become an accomplice. But you must do it in a detached manner, without hatred or anger. It's O.K. to defend yourself, and the reason the Dalai Lama tells his people to cool it with the Chinese is purely realistic: they are six million to the billion-plus Han.

"I always thinking entire humanity as one," he went on. "National status is not so important. But under present circumstances I am concerned about identity of Tibet and other small nations. We must distinguish between temporary and long-term goals. Long-term goal is that whole world become one nation. Short-term goal is self-determination for all individual states. In a family, many brothers and sisters living together. For harmony, each individual identity must be fully respected. But extreme individualism neglects others' rights and will bring disaster. Too much self-centered, lose genuine friend. During Korean War, Asians got impression that Americans were champions of liberty and democracy. That image disappeared due to certain politicians' actions. When only interested in self-interest, begin to lose friends. Cooperation is a genuine human quality. The other way, one nation exploit the others — a new type of colonialism. But the world economic situation will teach us our future.

"From Buddhist stand-point, if a national struggle is purely political and not spiritual, it is hard to justify. But our struggle is not only political, it is for preservation of the dharma, and preservation of Tibetan culture is indirectly of benefit to China, Buddhism not alien religion to China.

"For Tibetans, present time is the worst and darkest period of our whole history. In this century greatest number of humans killed, and techniques of destruction immensely increased. This has been the most complicated century in human history. We learned much and became more mature. It is human nature, when facing desperate situation, to use more intelligence. I believe next century will be happier."

An hour later, we had turned from the problems of the world to some of the more esoteric aspects of the religion, like the trance walkers, or *lamas lung gompas,* who having mastered wind meditation are said to be able to cover great distances in buoyant, bounding leaps, streaking at forty to fifty miles an hour completely tranced out. He told me about an old nun who claimed to have watched two highly realized hermits fly a hundred meters from one rock to another. "We believe training of mind, mental force, can overpower physical elements, and these unusual feats not so impossible."

Just as it was starting to get interesting, Tenzin Geyche Tethong ended the audience. The next group, some recent arrivals from Tibet, was waiting. We went into the other room, where they began prostrating. Among them I recognized Lobsang, red-cheeked nun with the gold eyetooth and the irrepressible smile whom I'd interviewed in Kathmandu two weeks before. Not daring to look up, she didn't recognize me. This was the first time any of them had set eyes on their ruling archangel, and he was there for them, as he had been for me. Leaning humbly, attentively, over the bowed group, he told them. "Work hard, study hard. Now you are in exile, but you are free."

Epilogue

A rch Steele's travels abroad as a foreign correspondent were legendary and well-documented. Five years ago, when he became legally blind, he found places nearer to home to investigate.

At age eighty-six, for instance, he hiked twelve miles to the bottom of the west end of the Grand Canyon, the Havasupai Indian Village. He was very excited with the beauty of Havasupai; the waterfalls and tropical growth amazed him.

Arch would feel the leaves and bark of the trees and want minute descriptions of the things he found difficult to see. His sense of touch was so acute he could identify most trees and plants by feeling the texture of bark, leaf or petal.

A few months before the Havasupai trip we had taken the mule trip to Phantom Ranch at the bottom of the Grand Canyon, a long, exciting trip for anyone and a daring undertaking for us eighty-plus adventurers.

Arch was not content to stay at home. In September of 1992 Arch realized he had never been to New Zealand or Australia, so off we went for a month-long odyssey of that wonderful (down under) part of the world, with both Tahiti and Fiji visited briefly.

In June 1991, a call came from Peggy and Tillman Durden (old friends from the days Till and Arch were with the New York Times Shanghai Bureau in China). The Durdins casually mentioned they had never been to the north rim of the Grand Canyon. We were on our way in a few days.

One night a television travelogue tempted us with great views of Rainbow Arch at Lake Powell. With no time wasted, we left home without reservations and marked off one more world wonder he had managed to see.

Arch was concerned for the preservation of our world and for the people and wild life on it. He sponsored and funded help for young journalists through his Alma Mater, Stanford University. He also donated acreage in Portal, Arizona to the Nature Conservancy as a tribute to his late wife, Esther Johnson Steele.

Most of Arch's papers are at Arizona State University in Tempe, Arizona, under the A.T. Steel Collection. While they were in the Orient, he and Esther collected many valuable and beautiful artifacts, which have been donated to the Heard Museum in Phoenix under the A.T. and Esther Steele Collection and can be enjoyed by many people.

His interest in world affairs never waned and during the Tiananmen Square tragedy in China, he followed every news release with sorrow and anger. Six months before his death, Arch told me about his trip to Llasa, Tibet, and showed me some wonderful pictures he had taken. I was fascinated with his description of this beautiful, once-peaceful country that he grieved for. Fortunately something is being done right now, as you can see in the information provided by the International

Campaign for Tibet in the Appendix.

The stories Arch wrote from and about Llasa, Tibet, unfolded in seven installments in the Rotogravure section of the Chicago Daily News in 1944. I thought it would be nice to re-publish them with his wonderful pictures for his family and friends. I suggested he call Arizona State University in Tempe, Arizona, and request copies. The university responded and we had the copies in our hands within a week.

After reading the story I realized this was going to be a project that could not be rushed. Unfortunately Arch's health was deteriorating fast. He had undergone surgery for cancer. We used the time spent at the Scottsdale Mayo Clinic for radiation therapy for research and writing.

Although the project gave him pleasure, his concentration and energy levels were very low and his spirit was light. We were very near the end of our efforts when he died. I promised him I would continue until I brought our efforts to their conclusion.

I regret he did not see his final contribution completed. He hoped his efforts in some small way would help Tibet. That is now in the hands of the Powers that be.

In October, while the forests were at their dazzling peak of changing colors, my grandson, Ric Quayle, and I took his remains to the north rim of the Grand Canyon. There at his favorite spot, Cape Royal, I emptied the container over the rim, letting the winds have their way with his ashes. As I did so, I murmered his Tibetan prayer, "Om mani padme hum." (Hail the Jewel of the Lotus)

I learned much from this man. We both felt that our meeting was not by accident, but by Providence. I thank the Celestial Custodians for the years we were together. Our years together were a time of growing, not aging. Arch Steele, born June 1902, was a joy to be with and a constant explorer. On February 26, 1992, he left without me to explore new territory. I miss him.

Bea Baker 1992

APPENDIX

Tibet at a glance . . .

SIZE	2.5 million sq. km.
CAPITAL	Lhasa.
POPULATION	6 million Tibetans , an estimated 7.5 million Chinese, most of whom are in Kham and Amdo.
RELIGION	Tibetan population is up to 99% Buddhist.
LANGUAGE	Tibetan (of the Tibeto-Burmese language family). The official language is Chinese.
STAPLE FOOD	Tsampa (roasted barley flour).
NATIONAL DRINK	Salted butter tea.
TYPICAL ANIMALS	Wild yak, Bharal (blue) sheep, Musk deer, Tibetan antelope, Tibetan gazelle, Kyang (wild ass), Pica.
TYPICAL BIRDS	Black necked crane, Lammergeier, Great crested grebe, Barheaded goose, Ruddy shel duck, Ibis-bill.
MAJOR ENVIRONMENTAL PROBLEMS	Rampant deforestation in eastern Tibet; poaching of large mammals.
AVERAGE ALTITUDE	14,000 feet.
HIGHEST MOUNTAIN	Chomo Langma (Mt. Everest) 29,028 feet.
AVERAGE RAINFALL	Varies widely . In the west it is 1 mm in January to 25 mm.in July.In the east, it is 25-50 in January and 800 in July.
AVERAGE TEMPERATIJRE	July 58f; January 24f.
MINERAL DEPOSITS	Borax, uranium, iron, chromite, gold
MAJOR RIVERS	Mekong, Yangtse, Salween, Tsangpo, Yellow
ECONOMY	**Tibetans:** predominantly agriculture and animal husbandry. **Chinese:** predominantly government, commerce and the service sector.
PROVINCES	U-Tsang (Central Tibet) Amdo (N.E. Tibet), Kham (S.E. Tibet).
BORDERING COUNTRIES	India, Nepal, Bhutan, Burma, China.
NATIONAL FLAG	Snow lions/red and blue rays. Outlawed in Tibet.
POLITICAL AND RELIGIOUS LEADER	The 14th Dalai Lama; in exile in Dharamsala, India.
GOVERNMENT IN EXILE	Parliamentary.
GOVERNMENT	Communist.
RELATIONSHIP WITH THE P.R.C.	Colonial.

1518 K Street, NW, Suite 410,
Washington DC 20005-1401
Tel. (202) 628-4123
Fax (202)347-6825

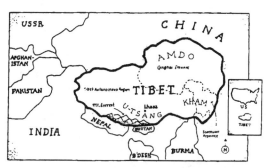

Tibet in Exile at a glance . . .

POPULATION	Total: 130,000. (In India 100,000; Nepal 25,000; Bhutan 2,000; Switzerland 2,000; Canada 500; United States 500.)
GOVERNMENT	Democratic. Popular & electoral college voting systems.
HEAD OF STATE	His Holiness the Dalai Lama.
CABINET LEVEL	Education, Finance, Health, Home Affairs, Information & International Relations, Religion & Culture & Security.
ELECTIONS	Assembly & Cabinet elections every 5 years.
SEAT OF GOVERNMENT	Dharamsala, northern India.
INT'L GOV'T OFFICES	Geneva, Kathmandu, London, New Delhi, New York, Tokyo, Zurich.
GOV'T EMPLOYEES	Over 1300.
GOV'T PUBLICATIONS	Sheja (Tibetan), Tibetan Bulletin, News Tibet (English), Tibbat Bulletin (Hindi), Actualites Tibetaines (French).
INDEPENDENT PUBLICATIONS	Mangtso, Da-sar, Da-sa Phongya, Rangzen (Tibetan). Xizang Luntan (Chinese), Tibetan Review, Rangzen (English).
LITERACY	Estimated at 60%.
MILITARY & POLICE	None.
GOVERNMENT INCOME	Annual voluntary tax, business revenue, donations.
NATIONAL FLAG	A mountain with snow lions & red and blue rays over sun.
NATIONAL HOLIDAYS	March 10-Uprising day; July 7-Birthday of the Dalai Lama; Sept. 2- Democracy Day; New Year (date changes).
MAJOR INSTITUTIONS	Institute of Performing Arts, Library, School of Dialectics, Medical Institute, Institute of Higher Tibetan Studies.
TIBETAN NGOs	Women's Organization, Youth Congress.
LANGUAGE	Tibetan. The host country's language is also spoken.
RELIGION	The overwhelming majority are Tibetan Buddhists. Some remain Bonpos. A very few are Christians and Muslims.
HEALTH PROBLEMS	Tuberculosis, malaria and gastro-intestinal ailments .
ECONOMY	Agriculture, agro-industrial, handicrafts, small business, carpet weaving.
LEGAL STATUS	Stateless. A small percentage of Tibetans bear foreign passports. Most hold Indian registration certificates.

1518 K Street, NW, Suite 410,
Washington DC 20005-1401
Tel. (202) 628-4123
Fax (202)347-6825

October 1991

ORGANIZATIONAL PROFILE

Mission:

The International Campaign for Tibet (ICT) is a nonpartisan, public interest group dedicated to promoting human rights and democratic freedoms for the people of Tibet. Founded in 1988, ICT is based in Washington, D.C., and is a tax-exempt, non-profit member-ship organization under Section 501 (c) (3) of the U.S. Tax Code.

ICT's principal activities include human rights advocacy, publishing reports and bulletins, testifying before Congressional bodies, conducting fact-finding missions, outreach to the public, serving as a Tibetan resource center, fact-checking materials for the media and other advocacy groups and lobbying for legislation (to the extent allowed by law).

Philosophy:

The International Campaign for Tibet operates from the belief that:

- governments and people around the world deserve accurate information on current conditions in Tibet;
- Tibet is a colony controlled by Chinese officials and from where natural resources are being rapidly extracted and taken to China;
- Tibetans are a "people" under international law and have the right to self-determination;
- The government of the P.R.C. has additional human rights obligations in Tibet based on the fact that Tibet is an occupied country which has a distinct language, culture and religion;
- Dialogue between the Tibetans and Chinese is an integral process towards finding solutions to the Tibet question.

Projects:

Human Rights Project — monitors and investigates human rights conditions and then works with appropriate organizations and government officials to publicize abuses and bring pressure to bear on the government of the PRC. This year, ICT is focusing on 10 Tibetan prisoners of conscience who represent thousands of Tibetans who remain imprisoned.

Legislative Activities — center on marshalling support for Tibet in the form of letters from members of Congress to the P.R.C. leadership, floor speeches, testimony, resolutions and legislation. ICT also responds to many requests from members of Congress and their staff for information and assistance.

Fact-Finding Missionss — ICT conducts on-site fact-finding missions to Tibet, China, India and Nepal. ICT's most recent mission was in eastern Tibet investigating the Chinese population transfer, education of Tibetan children and deforestation .

Environmental Projects — In conjunction with World Wildlife Fund, the Campaign initiated a scholarship program to send Tibetans to environmental training programs in the United States and elsewhere. The project promotes the idea that traditional Tibetan relationships with the natural environment should be restored in Tibet.

The Nepal Project — focuses on protecting the right of Tibetan refugees to safely pass through Nepal. ICT has coordinated strong responses to the Nepalese government on several occasions when Tibetans were forcibly *refouled* from Nepal.

The China Project — networks with exiled Chinese democracy and overseas Chinese organizations, works with Chinese language media, edits and translates books and materials and conducts research on methods of Chinese rule of Tibet. The project also funnels Chinese language material on Tibet into China.

Education & Publications — ICT's bi-monthly Tibet Press Watch is distributed to all prominent organizations and individuals who are engaged in work on Tibet. ICT published the leading report on religious persecution as well as a handbook on the Tibetan environment. ICT staff regularly give lectures and provide news and background to the media.

Successes:

- Organized the Dalai Lama's 1991 Washington visit, during which he met President Bush and Congressional leaders.

- Lobbied for the passage of legislation providing for the Tibetan Voice of America service, visas for Tibetan immigrants to the U.S. and Fulbright scholarships for Tibetan refugees.

- Organized an international conference for groups working in areas of Tibetan human rights, refugee relief and cultural.

- Secured meetings with editorial boards of leading newspapers resulting in heightened media coverage.

Staff:

Lodi G. Gyari, President; John Ackerly, Projects Director and Legal Counsel;
Jigme Ngagpo, Political Analyst; Monica Garry, Assistant; Gyaltsen Tsering, Intern;
Patrick Doherty, Intern.

1518 K Street, NW, Suite 410, Washington, DC 20005-1401.
Tel. (202) 628-4123
Fax (202) 347-6825

A Searchlight on the other Tianamen Square

It's a cruel irony that in a country whose exiled leader, the Dalai Lama, is pacifism incarnate, an estimated 1.2 million people have died due to foreign occupation. Add in the plundering of monasteries and the annihilation of forests and animals, and you have the tragically simple history of Tibetan hardship at the hands of the Chinese for the past 42 years.

But there is a glimmer of good news: The Dalai Lama's declaration of 1991 as the Year of Tibet turned out to be far more than just optimistic marketing, thanks in part to a stateside human-rights group known as the International Campaign for Tibet. Lobbying by ICT has helped bring about a dramatic shift in U.S. policy toward the Chinese occupation. Congress has at last broken years of official indifference by acknowledging Tibet to be an illegally occupied nation whose legitimate government is in exile. Even more significant in the complex shadow-dance between Washington and Beijing, President Bush received the Dalai Lama in his private White House quarters last April 16 — an unprecedented meeting that outraged Chinese officials.

ICT was founded in 1988 by a Tibetan named Tenzin Tethong with the help of an American climber and attorney named John Ackerly, who, on a visit to Lhasa the year before, had been shot at, detained, and interrogated by Chinese troops. In the years since, it has acted as nerve center for a whole range of Tibetan issues — circulating Amnesty International-style alerts about Tibetan political prisoners in China, jump-starting a Voice of America radio frequency for Tibet, and creating environmental scholarship programs here in the states.

"The crucial moment for Tibet is going to be when communism falls in China," says Galen Rowell, whose photographs accompany the Dalai Lama's text in the 1990 book *My Tibet.* "The great fear is that even a democratic China could contrive to hold onto Tibet; the world must be ready. ICT's role is to turn up the voltage — and that's just what it's doing."

by John Ackerly

August 6. 1991

UNITED NATIONS PASSES TIBET HUMAN RIGHTS RESOLUTION

The United Nations Human Rights Sub-Commission passed a resolution on Friday, August 23, criticizing China's record of human rights violations in Tibet. The resolution said that China's violations of fundamental human rights "threaten the distinct cultural, religious and national identity of the Tibetan people."

This event marks the first time that the United Nations has addressed the issue of Tibet since 1965. The General Assembly passed three resolutions condemning China's policies in Tibet in l959, 1961 and 1965. China became a member of the United Nations in 1971.

None of China's usual allies — previously led by Cuba and Pakistan — made an attempt to amend the text or block the vote by a procedural device. The resolution was initially sponsored by sub-commission members from Holland and the Philippines. The sub-commission is made up of experts from 26 countries, including China, the United States, India and the Soviet Union.

The resolution requests the Secretary General to transmit information about the situation in Tibet to the Commission on Human Rights, which meets in Geneva each February.

The Dalai Lama, who was in Europe when the resolution passed, hailed it as a triumph for truth. He also spoke optimistically about events in the Soviet Union and their implications for China and Tibet.

International Campaign for Tibet President Lodi Gvari, who is also the Dalai Lama's Special Envoy for United Nations Affairs, attended the sub-commission meeting to personally appeal to the members of the sub-commission. Mr. Gyari said, "this is a significant moment for Tibet — Tibet is once again on the formal agenda of the United Nations." ICT Legal Counsel John Ackerly attended the first week of the sub-commission to present a report on the ICT fact-finding mission to eastern Tibet, conducted during the summer. ICT specifically prepared a report for the sub-commission based on its first hand observations of conditions inside Tibet.

Gvari also commented that this resolution "was particularly difficult for the Chinese coming, as it did, with the failure of the hardliner's coup in Moscow and the imminent separation of the Baltic states."

China Condemns Resolution

The day after the UN passed the resolution the New China News Agency denounced it as "illegal and null and void and absolutely unacceptable to the Chinese government." The statement further said that the resolution "goes against the principals of respecting state sovereignty and non-interference in the internal affairs of countries enshrined in the U.N. charter and international law."

While the resolution did not directly address issues of sovereignty, it spoke of Tibet's "national identity," which China, and others, appeared to take as a reference to self-determination.

TEXT OF CONGRESSIONAL RESOLUTION DECLARING TIBET AN OCCUPIED COUNTRY
OCTOBER 3,1991

SEC. 355. CHINA'S ILLEGAL CONTROL OF TIBET

It is the sense of the Congress that—

(1) Tibet, including those areas incorporated into the Chinese provinces of Sichuan, Yunnan, Gansu, and Quinghai, is an occupied country under the established principles of international law-

(2) Tibet's true representatives are the Dalai Lama and the Tibetan Government in exile as recognized by the Tibetan people;

(3) Tibet has maintained throughout its history a distinctive and sovereign national, cultural, and religious identity separate from that of China and, except during periods of illegal Chinese occupation, has maintained a separate and sovereign political and territorial identity;

(4) Historical evidence of this separate identity may be found in Chinese archival documents and traditional dynastic histories, in United States recognition of Tibetan neutrality during World War II, and in the fact that a number of countries including the United States, Mongolia, Bhutan, Sikkim, Nepal, India, Japan, Great Britain, and Russia recognized Tibet as an independent nation or dealt with Tibet independently of any Chinese government;

(5) In 1949-1950, China launched an armed invasion of Tibet in contravention of international law;

(6) It is the policy of the United States to oppose aggression and other illegal uses of force by one country against the sovereignty of another as a manner of acquiring territory, and to condemn violations of international law, including the illegal occupation of one country by another; and

(7) Numerous United States declarations since the Chinese invasion have recognized Tibet's right to self-determination and the illegality of China's occupation of Tibet.

United States Congress Declares Tibet an Occupied Country

Washington, D.C., October 29, 1991

The United States Congress has declared Tibet an "occupied country" whose "true representatives are the Dalai Lama and the Tibetan Government in exile." The bill was part of the State Department Authorization Act which President Bush signed yesterday, on October 28.

The President, who met with the Dalai Lama in April, is travelling to Asia in November, but is not planning on stopping in Beijing. According to Congressional staff, the State Department did little to lobby against the bill.

The bill notes that numerous declarations by the United States since the 1949 Chinese invasion of Tibet have recognized Tibet's right to self-determination and the illegality of China's occupation. However, since the early 1970's the United States government has done little to recognize the plight of Tibet.

Lodi Gyari, President of the International Campaign for Tibet, called the legislation "an historic triumph for the struggle of the Tibetan people for self-determination. It is so heartening that after all these years, governments are again beginning to seriously address the tragic situation of Tibet."

The Chinese government issued a strongly worded condemnation when the bill was introduced, stating that "this constitutes an act of tramping upon the established norm in international relations and wanton interference in China's internal affairs." An editorial following the official denunciation advised Congressman Gilman (R-NY), the original sponsor of the bill, "to shut his mouth."

The bill was widely supported in both the House and the Senate. In the Senate, the bill was introduced by the Chairman of the Foreign Relations Committee, Senator Pell (D-RI) along with Senators Helms (R-NC) and Moynihan (D-NY). In the House, the bill was backed by a broad coalition of members including Berman (D-CA), Dymally (D-CA), Gejdenson (D-CT), Gilman (R-NY), Lantos (D-CA), Porter (R-IL) and Rose (D-NC).

Other portions of the bill are significant, such as the definition of

Tibet. The bill states that Tibet includes those areas incorporated into the Chinese provinces of Sichuan, Yunnan, Gansu and Qinghai. China officially defines Tibet as a much smaller area known as the Tibet Autonomous Region, which includes less than half of the Tibetans living under China's control. Congress cites historical evidence of Tibet's separate identity from Chinese archival documents and traditional dynastic histories, United States recognition of Tibetan neutrality during World War II, among many other factors.

This bill comes just two months after the United Nations Human Rights Subcommission passed a resolution expressing concern at the threat to "the distinct cultural, religious and nations identity of the Tibetan people."